All the
Write Pieces

An anthology of pieces by members of
Retford Writers' Group

They come from across the country to meet in
North Nottinghamshire

The Lime Press

Some of these pieces have previously appeared on the website,
www. retwords.wordpress.com
where 300 more pieces can be viewed.

Published by

The Lime Press
1 Lime Grove
Retford
DN22 7YH

Printed in England by
CLOC Ltd
London N17 9QU

All the Write Pieces

CONTENTS

These pieces have been selected by the members of Retford Writers' Group and their own works grouped together. The sequence of writers is random. The ethos of the group is simply to enjoy writing and sharing it.

No works were originally intended for publication. However, after meeting for seven years, we feel that many pieces are worth sharing and hope that everyone will find something to enjoy in this treasury.

Retford Writers' Group is an open group, which meets at Retford Library, Nottinghamshire and everyone is welcome.

Contact can be made through Lime Press, or the website https://retwords.wordpress.com, or the library: 01777 708724

Kaye Locke 1
- Foreboding
- Released
- The Shape of Love

Michael Keeble 7
- Kings
- Trainers
- The Dragon (and George)

Margaret Moreton 21
- Wild Words
- Star
- Surreal

Kevin Murphy 27
- Dirty Deeds Done Good
- For my Father on his Anniversary
- The Big Derby

Rachel Hilton 39
- Just be careful
- Paris
- Time

Pete Brammer 43
- Old Ned and Flo
- Elvis in my life
- An Empty Stage

Angela O'Connor   51
  • Cabin ten
  • Piccadilly Abode ,
  • The Life Model.

David R Graham   54
  • Sterling Stuff
  • The Cold Rain Fell
  • False Awakening

Barrie Purnell   63
  • Free Verse
  • Scarborough Steps
  • Are you Happy?

Faymarie Morris.   70
  • Falling in Love takes
    more than a Kiss
  • The Picture
  • To Someone who
    Cares

Robert Tansey   76
  • The Past/the
    Present/the Future
  • Ode to a towpath
    spring
  • One summer's
    evening

Pat Barnett   81
  • Emergency
  • Snowdrops
  • Lumiere 15

Michael Healy   84
  • The Words that we Use
  • The Pestilential Little Mouse
  • Down in the Land of Lingtong
    Boodle

Cynthia Smith   88
  • My secret place
  • Shop!

Chris South   93
  • Born From Nought
  • The Clear Out
  • My Cuppa Runneth Over (In
    Strictest Confidence!) excerpt

Sarah Bowden: 100
  • Extract from a work in progress

Foreboding

I'm picking at the thread
of my doubts and fears
The old worn-out sweater of
optimism no longer offers comfort
Now rough and scratchy
it torments me

Even the night-time promise
of refuge is broken
Sheets are cold and harsh
and the charcoal night
only lights the fires of dread
My eyes won't shut

I watch the subtleties of change
And hope they are nothing
But the turnings of a ball
That the stitches won't drop
And there will be no
unravelling

Kaye Locke

Released

It's early. Still dark. But the dog is insistent and if I don't crawl out of bed now she'll probably make a mess on the floor. She's getting old now and her bladder isn't what it used to be.

As I flip-flop down the stairs, I remember what day it is and a shiver passes through my body.

'Someone walking over your grave' my mother would have said.

I open the back door on to a world of white. Another dump of snow in the night. The dog almost disappears as she leaps into it with glee, her paw prints criss-crossing the garden in a crazy zig-zag of joy.

I leave her out there while I put the kettle on and try to liven myself up.

Sipping my tea and watching the slow glow of morning creep in through the closed curtains, I try not to think too hard about the day ahead. I'm supposed to be happy. It's supposed to be a red letter day. My husband is coming home.

He's been away for four years. Getting out early for good behaviour. I wonder if he's going to be able to get here with the weather as it is. I'm not going to pick him up. No. He understood. I'm sure he understood.

The dog comes in and unsuccessfully tries to leap on to my lap shaking snow from her coat and nearly spilling my tea as she does so. I shout at her, probably more fiercely than I should have and she slinks off and sits in her basket looking at me with her unblinking soulful eyes.

Sorry' I say out loud, and pat her on the head. That's all she needs. That's all it takes sometimes, even with humans. Just a quick and heartfelt 'sorry', and the equivalent of a pat on the head. I dunno, a hug maybe, or just a smile.

I drag myself up the stairs and stand under the shower for a full five minutes, washing off the night with my 'Japanese Spa' shower gel. I don't know what's so Japanese about it, I got it from the supermarket

2

up the road. Anyway, it does the trick, I feel fresher once I've dried and put some clean clothes on.

I wasn't sure what to wear. Should I try to look nice? Be welcoming? Or just look myself, in my old jeans and tatty jumper? I decide on the latter. It's how he'll remember me.

He's not coming until the afternoon.

'not sure what time' he said, in our brief phone conversation 'depends on the trains.'

I don't know much about the trains. Haven't been on one in years. I get a bit claustrophobic on public transport, it's why I love my little car so much. She's been a godsend. Oh yes, it's a she. I feel safe in her, comfortable and in control. In fact, some times, on the bad nights, I go out to the drive and just sit in her, lock the doors and turn on the radio. She is my mother ship..

The morning slips by in a haze of dog walking, dusting, changing the bed, and hoovering. Before I know it, it is lunchtime, but I can't eat anything, the mere thought of food sends me dry heaving over the toilet. It won't do me any harm I suppose, I could probably do with losing a few pounds. It's easy to eat rubbish when you're on your own, and I'm sure my shape change won't go unmentioned.

I watch the news at 1:00. To my mock horror they don't mention the imminent release of my spouse. Amazing how such momentous events in a life can go completely unnoticed by the rest of the world.

I switch off the TV and let the dog out in the back garden again. There's a weak sun and the dog's paw prints are losing their shape as the top layer of snow begins to melt. The cold is refreshing and I suck in the dry winter air as if it's my last gasp.

I don't know what to do with myself for the rest of the afternoon. I try to paint, but the inspiration isn't there and the paints won't move on the paper as willingly as they usually do. Then I pick up my kindle. That's been a godsend, I read so many books, mostly psychological thrillers and murder mysteries. It seems a bit counter-intuitive, but I

3

enjoy those more than the foolish romantic stuff women of my age are supposed to read. Nonetheless, today I find the words swim about and even though I read the same page umpteen times, I can't make sense of it.

It's half past three, and getting dark already. I prayed and prayed that he would arrive in daylight, but it doesn't look like that's going to happen. But then I hear a car grinding to a halt outside. It's a taxi.

Should I go and open the door, or wait for him to knock? I don't want him to think I've been waiting, waiting, waiting, like I have, so I leave it and listen for the once familiar four raps. I stand in the kitchen, my legs feel numb, my breath is sharp staccato, and I feel slightly dizzy. Then the doorbell rings.

I reach out to the worktop, then take a deep breath, before walking as calmly as I can to the door. I can see his shape through the glass. Instantly recognisable. He's tall, quite lanky really, and I can see a halo of curly hair outlined against the setting sun.

'Took yer time' he says, as I open the door.

I see him briefly appraising me.

'Christ, I'd fergotten how bloody old you are and you've been piling on the pounds I see.', he says, as he tries to push past me.

Instinctively I put my hand up against his chest, in a 'halt' motion. My body is on auto pilot.

'yeah, pleased to see you too' he says in his old familiar sarcastic way. 'get outta the way woman, and go and get kettle on'.

I look him straight in his steely eyes, my body definitely in auto pilot, and say 'No'.

Just like that.

'No'.

It confuses him. Of course it does. He snatches at my wrist to tug my hand away, but all of a sudden I'm quick and nimble. The dog is snapping at his ankles and he looks down and kicks at her. It gives me enough time to deftly bring my other hand up, the one with the kitchen knife in it, and slash at his turkey neck.

As he crumples, he looks surprised. He shouldn't be.

Kaye Locke

The Shape of Love

There are no corners to hide in
And no straight paths
or sides to take

There is no long and short
Nor tip of the iceberg
Or points to make

No, Love is a circle
Delicious, curvaceous
A two tier cream cake

A full harvest moon
A banging drum heart
A promise you make

A ring on your finger
A cuff on your wrist
A hunger that wakes

A bowl full of spices
A bouncing beachball
That gives, and, that takes

Oh Love is a circle
A merry go round
Of tender heartaches

Yes, love is a circle
Two people conjoined
As endless soul mates

Unless, of course, it becomes a triangle…

Kaye Locke

Kings

When I was young I earned my keep as servant to a lord.
He worked me more and paid me less than he could well afford.
I tended to his clothing and his food and to his drink,
And left him on his own a lot so he could sit and think.
He said his wealth was in his mind; a wealth you cannot hold,
But I know best his wealth was real and counted out in gold.
My wealthy lord had wealthy friends and they too thought a lot
(So much to learn when you're a have and not a poor have not).
They'd call upon my master's house and join him in his thought,
Or study manuscripts they'd found, or papers that they'd brought.
"Ahmed" they'd call (for that's my name), "bring us some food and
drink.
"We need to be sustained with wine, and sweetmeats help us think."
Of course I served my master well, I had no other choice,
But none of it fulfilled my mind or made my soul rejoice.

And so these pampered learned lords would while away the day
With reading, and with thinking, and with nothing much to say
Until my master Melchior one day called out to me
"Go saddle up the camels; you'd better make it three.
"Victual up the caravan we'll be away a while
"And pack a bag yourself" he said "We're travelling in style."
That meant of course that I'd be there to dress and preen these fops,
As well as feed the camels at our, no doubt frequent, stops.
Earlier that afternoon around came Balthazar,
Who huddled up with Melchior to chat about some star.
Then Gaspar rushed excited in, and gabbled out the news
That Dan'el and Balaam had both foretold that all the Jews
Would get a new Messiah, or at least a brand new King;
That this, tied in with this new star, was really just the thing
They'd all been waiting for so long and time was now quite tight,
And they must all be saddled up and set to go tonight.

Of course, the preparations took me very many days,
And all my lords would do at night was hang around and gaze
Up in the sky into the west and stand around like fools,
Until at last I'd packed our bags and loaded all the mules.

Lord Gaspar and Lord Balthazar were very fancy friends
Who'd show off all their fine new gowns, and follow fashion trends,
And oh they loved their unctuants, their perfumes and pomade,
Unlike my own Lord Melchior, his tastes were rather staid.
His pref'rences could trace their roots way back to times of old,
Like many more before and since he kept his wealth in gold.
A mule was set aside for each of these three lords to load
With treasures of their choice alone before we hit the road.
Thus it was that Balthazar with frankincense did weigh
His mule to nearly breaking point, but who am I to say
That this was any worse than that of Gaspar who did pack
His mule with jars of Myrrh, while quite concealed inside a sack
Lord Melchior hid bars of gold and strapped them to a beast.
And thus our caravan was set from greatest and to least.
In spite of camels and of mules not one was I to ride;
My Lords climbed up upon their steeds and I walked on beside.

We travelled on at nights and sat to eat at break of dawn
And journeyed on awhile until the brightening sun had worn
A path to highest heavens then, beneath our shelt'ring tent,
We slept until the sun declined and once again had bent
His head below the earth, and then we travelled on
Until the sun rose up again and all the night had gone.

Before we slept these worthy lords would check their treasure trove
Ensuring that their wealth was there and that no sneaky cove
Had dipped a thieving hand inside and scooped some myrrh or gold
Or frankincense, though truth be known they would have needs been
bold
To get away with such a crime and realise it's worth

For these lords worshipped nought so well in heaven or on earth.
And so we travelled on until the star (it seemed to them)
Rested near a little town that's known as Bethlehem.
My lords consulted all their books, then thought and talked a bit,
And came to the conclusion that considering that it
Portended a new ruler for the kingdom, then the thing
To do most properly was tell the current king.
So (after checking on their wealth) we trudged a further night
And then far in the distance, and by daybreak's softest light
Jerusalem, King Herod's seat, appeared as silhouette
It's mighty temple still half built, the scaffold round it yet.
The caravan is called to halt, my lords they then dismount,
They talk awhile and then decide there's time enough to count
Their wealth again, and so each bag is lifted from its beast,
The contents emptied out and back from greatest and to least,
And then when it's accounted for and none has disappeared,
They call me to their side, and just as I had feared,
They tell me they would go alone and I must guard the loot,
And woe betide if any ounce or drop or strip or shoot,
Should be astray when they returned from meeting with the king,
And be assured that they would check by counting ev'rything.
So much for trusting me, I thought. These wise old fools have need
Of simple kindly sentiments to overcome their greed.
Enough of all my bitterness, suffice to say I burned
With anger at their attitudes, but then when they returned,
They checked their wealth again, and finding it all there,
They lay down in their tent to chat and ordered me prepare
A fine repast while they discussed the meeting with the King
Who'd greeted them all friendly like, and asked them please to bring
The news of where the new King lay so Herod could perforce
Pay homage to his substitute, preparing in due course
A fitting place for him to dwell and rule the lands around,
But asked them not to tell a soul about what they had found.
Well I'm not wise or learned in books and lack the very things
You need to understand the thoughts of rulers and of kings

9

But nonetheless I didn't think that any good would come
Of telling Herod what he asked; instead I just played dumb.

When night fell we were up again and following that star
A few more hours ride they said. It wasn't very far.
Not so far on camel's back I thought. That's fine for them,
But once more I stayed silent till we came to Bethlehem.

We came upon a humble house, on which the star shone down,
The same as many other humble houses in this town.
No battlements upon its roof, no guards beside the door,
And yet this was the house foretold, of that they were quite sure.
Lord Gaspar and Lord Balthazar quite lost their dignity.
They climbed down from their camels and laughed immod'rately.
Outside this little dwelling place, wherein was meant to be
The prophesied new Jewish King that they had come to see.
Lord Melchior frowned down on them, and in his quiet way,
Admonished them to calm themselves; consider how to pay
The rightful homage to a King whose birth had been foretold.
His own intent was to present a humble gift of gold.
The other two could not contain their shock at this proposed
Donation of his worldly wealth, and both were quite opposed
To giving up their unctuants and scents so dearly bought
To one whose humble dwelling wasn't quite a Royal Court.
They flounced and sulked and minced about; they just could not be sure,
Till Melchior with firm resolve just knocked upon the door.
Out came a lady, babe in arms, and both looked so serene
That all the lords dropped to their knees as if before a queen.
Nothing came to mind to do and nothing to be said,
So I too fell upon my knees and humbly bowed my head.
As if upon a gesture giv'n or at a sound unheard
My lords arose and turned about and then without a word
Approached their mules, still laden down with what they'd valued most

Unhitched them from the caravan and led them to our host.

Each lord unslung the treasure bags to each mule's great relief,
And then to my amazement and my utter disbelief,
The frankincense and myrrh and gold were laid before the Child
Who looking down from mother's arms just raised his hands and
smiled.
Well I was still on bended knee when She with holy grace
Asked me to rise, and I too saw the Baby's smiling face.
We said no more, but as one man, we slowly left that scene,
And none of us, not even I, forgot where we had been.

King Herod never learned from us where'er the baby lay
And I heard that the family left Judah on that day.
My lords still think a lot it seems and study hard to learn,
But now they give away a lot of ev'rything they earn.
Melchior no longer hoards his heavy bags of gold,
Lord Gaspar and lord Balthazar, unlike the days of old,
No longer crave their unctuants and incense as before,
Though they still love their finery and keep that all in store.
Myself I still serve Melchior, but he has set me free,
And when they all come round to ours I treat them all to tea.

Michael Keeble

Trainers

Johnny performed a few stretches in front of the mirror in the hallway watching himself critically as he did so. Not bad he thought, but then a pretty abstemious life had led to a pretty fit body and one that his last girlfriend had found desirable. It was a shame that Sarah had been so clingy; if she had simply enjoyed his company for what it was and what it offered, they might still be together instead of breaking up as they had last weekend. There were tears of course but they couldn't be helped and now he had this wonderful day to break in his new trainers with no worries about anyone getting in his way.

He stepped outside the front door, turned his face towards the sun feeling its gentle heat and started to run towards the nearby woods. By the time he had reached the edge of the woods he was already in rhythm. He could hear his breathing in time with the pad of his new trainers. They were feeling good on his feet.

He paused at the edge of the wood to fix his MP3 player earphones into his ears, selected a rock playlist and set it to loud. Right, he thought, here we go, let's see how the shoes manage off road. He entered the wood following the rutted track into the heart of this 30 acre patch of greenery. He became totally absorbed in his running and his thoughts. The music shut out the rest of the world and he was only vaguely aware of his surroundings. His thoughts flitted to the relationship that he had just ended. It was for the best. People just got in the way. He hardly got in touch with anyone these days except electronically and even email and the social networking sites got on his nerves now. He was happiest working from home on his computer and only meeting with real people when he absolutely had to, and at the end of a day with his computer, his nightly runs were the perfect relaxation.

He was really into his rhythm now and hardly felt the ground beneath his feet. The gentle breeze blew against his face drying his sweat before it had time to gather on his brow. His feet seemed to automatically jump over the ruts in the dirt track through the woods landing perfectly on the other side. He had run this way many times in his old trainers but they had become so worn that they had begun to hurt his feet. It was with great reluctance that he had gone to buy new trainers, hoping that he could buy an identical pair but inevitably finding that the manufacturers had stopped making that design. The specialist shop had recommended a pair at a considerable cost, but the assistant had reminded him that they would be worth every penny if they worked well. The thought had crossed his mind that they would be a waste of every penny if they hadn't worked but they had felt very good on his feet in the shop and he was secretly proud of the fact that he was such a committed runner that he needed to buy such an expensive pair.

As he ran his thoughts were interrupted by a niggling irritation in his right trainer. He had somehow picked up a stone and it was grinding against his heel. He ran on for a while hoping that it would somehow dislodge, but it was no good, it had ruined his mood. He stopped by the road, crouched down and took his trainer off.

****

Cass was really taken with Jake. She'd been out with other guys, stealing cars and driving around, but that had usually been at night and all they had done was drive around the estate in some beat up Escort or Fiesta or something. Jake was different, he knew how to drive fast; he could even handbrake turn. The last car before this one was a BMW and that could really travel. Cass loved the buzz of going fast and racing round corners. Jake always had some great stuff with him as well. When they'd finished with the car Jake always torched it in some out of the way place so that the law couldn't identify them. That meant a bit of a walk back but with Jake that was OK.

Cass had skipped out of school today and met up with Jake in the town. They had taken some stuff and hung around for a bit until Jake had suddenly said he was bored and that they should do something different. We need to nick a car he said, but not the usual crap, something else. He must have been thinking about it for a while because he said he knew what he wanted and where he could get it. He led her out of town a short way until they came to a tree lined street with cars parked all along it. There was no one about and he walked

13

up the middle of the road in that confident way he had. Cass walked on the pavement keeping pace with him saying nothing. She'd done this before. She kept an eye open for anyone coming up the pavement. Jake stopped opposite what looked like an old Land Rover that had been stripped of some of its body panels. It had an exhaust that pointed into the air and had very fat chunky tyres. Almost before she knew it, Jake was in the car with the engine running. She climbed up into the passenger seat and Jake let in the clutch and sped away down the road.

This was so different to the other cars that they had ridden in. It was very high off the ground and the ride was uncomfortably bouncy. Jake drove out of town towards the woods in the distance. He said that this car needed to be off road. Cass sat in the passenger seat mesmerised by Jake's handling of this strange vehicle. They drove along until they came to a ninety degree bend in the road beyond which were the woods. Instead of following the road Jake carried on at the same speed and crashed through the old wooden fence that bordered the wood. Cass screamed in delight and glanced over at Jake. He was grinning madly and fighting the steering wheel as the car bucked over the rough ground. He tried to maintain the speed, but realised that he could not manoeuvre round the trees unless he slowed down a bit. After a few minutes he came upon a track and steered the Land Rover onto it. He could get his speed up now and pushed the car as fast as he could, crashing through undergrowth and breaking saplings as he went. The car hit a large tree a glancing blow and shook them both about a bit but they weren't hurt. Cass took out two cigarettes and lit one of them with a lot of difficulty, partly because of the bouncing of the car and partly because she couldn't stop giggling. When she had managed to light the first cigarette she leaned over to place it in Jake's mouth, but just as he opened his mouth for it, the car gave a huge jolt and she dropped the cigarette in his lap. Jake took his hands of the wheel and patted at his lap to knock the burning cigarette onto the floor. Cass joined in, giggling. Without Jake's hands on the wheel the car bucked and weaved all over the track bouncing off trees and throwing them all over the cabin of the car. Jake managed to get a grip on the wildly spinning steering wheel and slowed the Land Rover to a stop. He clambered out of the cab and looked back where they had been. They had rutted the soft earth and there were signs of damage on a number of the trees and rather absurdly, a single trainer lying by the side of the track. He got back into the Land Rover and joined Cass who was still giggling. He drove more carefully out of the woods and headed for a country lane not far from the town. He set fire to the car and they started to walk back.

******

Johnny never heard the Land Rover coming and never felt the impact as it flung him through the trees and scrub to lie half in and half out of a ditch some ten feet from the edge of the track. When he came to, he felt the pain in his head but couldn't seem to move. He passed out again.

When he came round again darkness had fallen. He felt no real pain, but was cold and frightened. He was thirsty. How long was it you could live without water? Someone would find him. This was the UK for goodness sake; people didn't have accidents and then not get found. But how will anyone know he was here. He wasn't on the track and there may be no sign that he had ever been in these woods. There was his trainer. He remembered. He had stopped to shake a stone from his shoe. He had taken his shoe off and then whatever happened had happened. His trainer will be out there; a brand new expensive trainer. Someone will notice it and investigate. He drifted off into unconsciousness again.

When he came round again it was day. He was aware of how dry his mouth felt, and how disorientated he felt. His mind wandered into the most bizarre daydreams. All he could see was the branches of the trees above him. He watched the birds and could hear them talking to each other. He could see two magpies talking to each other. Was it two for joy? Someone would come. He could hear the rooks in the trees above him cawing as if they were a concert orchestra. He imagined that he could hear the melody as it washed over him. They were all calling for help for him. Why was no one listening? The magpies had come down from the tree and were walking towards him. Magpies have such purposeful walks. One came right up to his head. He could just see him if he turned his eyes to the extreme left. The other one hopped onto his chest and cocked his head sideways to look at him. He couldn't watch both of them together. He felt a sharp peck on his left ear. He turned his eyes to the left again and the magpie moved away cautiously. He felt a peck on his chin. He turned his eyes on the magpie on his chest which moved to the right side of his head. This wasn't really happening, he was just imagining it. A peck on his left ear, then on his right ear. Moving his eyes kept them back. He must keep moving his eyes. They were afraid to attack him while he was alive. He kept his eyes open and watched the magpies.

Michael Keeble

The Dragon (and George)

The story of St George is of a brave and noble Knight,
Who saves a Princess in distress by offering to fight
A dragon, armed with nothing but a horse, a shield and spear,
And then, with God upon his side, and therefore naught to fear
He overcomes the beast at last, returns the Maid unhurt
And for these deeds takes this reward: to preach, maybe convert
The town to Christianity, and having thus his say,
He girds himself in red crossed cloak and softly rides away

Well that's what legend's telling us about his little brawl.
That's the story, here's the truth, from one who saw it all.

George was just a little boy when he came to Honah-Lee.
I was lying in my cave when he first encountered me.
There aren't so many visit, so I was quite surprised
To be presented with a child so ripe to terrorise.
I started with a little smoke (that often makes them quake)
But this lad kept on coming; not a tremor or a shake.
Next I tried a flash of flame to really make him think
He didn't even falter once, nor did he even blink
But came and hugged my horny head and scratched behind my ear,
And told me he would be my friend for ever and a year

Well so it was. We stayed good friends and always kept in touch.
When he was far away from me I missed him very much.
He'd come into my cave at nights; we'd chat until the dawn.
I'd tell him of the hundred years that passed since I was born
He'd tell me of the places he had been since last we met,
And talk of things he dreamed about that hadn't happened yet.

One day he told about a king with wealth beyond compare,
Whose daughter was a beauteous maid with golden flowing hair.

He warmed his hands upon my breath and then before me laid
A cunning plan to part this king from riches and from maid.
We would arrive at dead of night when all were fast asleep,
And I would roar and be quite fierce and eat up all the sheep.
"OK so far", I said, "but wait, there's one thing's got it beat.
"In spite of what they say you know us dragons don't eat meat"
"We'll hide the sheep" said George at last "and let them think it's you
"Perception is reality. To them it will be true.
"Then you declare a comely maid of royal blood's your taste,
"And if you don't get one right soon you'll lay the land to waste.
"Along I come and tell the king that I'm the man to rid
"His kingdom of the nasty worm, and then I'll make my bid
"For half his wealth, his daughter's hand and named as his sole heir
And we will live in luxury without a single care."
"Hold on," says I "Am I the worm referred to in this plan?
"You know that as we're firmest friends I'll help you if I can,
"But do I have to be a worm? It seems to denigrate.
"My pref'rence would be 'dragon' when you two negotiate
"The terms of my demise and then the dowry for your bride,
"And hopefully, for me, a little something on the side."

The planning done and terms agreed we flew away anon,
Arriving in the dead of night when all the folk had gone.
We rounded up the sheep and put them in a lonely byre,
And then I landed on a hill and roared and breathed out fire,
Demanding princesses for lunch and threatening the worst
And trying to assure the King that all his land was cursed.
Our George meanwhile gained audience and followed up his plan:
Convincing of his Majesty that he's the only man
That can defeat this dreadful *worm* (He really did mean me),
And happy to achieve this feat for one quite modest fee.
These terms set out in simple words, he waited for assent,
But got instead a swift repost and major ego dent.
The King it seemed was not so green as he had seemed to be
And called the bluff of our brave George, and by extension me.

He staked his pretty maiden girl upon a far off hill,
And sent a challenge back to me to do just what I will.
Well I have no more appetite for maidens than for sheep,
So I slunk off a mile or so to sooth myself in sleep.
When I woke up I found that George was standing by my side,
And with him was the Princess that he wanted as his bride.
He said he needed help again to make his dream come true,
And while I listened carefully he told me what we'd do.
He tied a rope around my neck and led me into town,
I walked as if I was subdued, my head was hanging down.
The Princess held his hand so tight and looked at him with eyes
That brimmed with adoration for the man who'd cut her ties.
The three of us took up our place in front of City Hall,
The crowds were gathered in the square and George addressed them all
"You people see what I have done that your fine King denied.
"I have subdued this fierce beast and maybe could have died,
"Your beauteous Princess I have saved from dragon's tooth and claws,
"The Lord thy God was on my side and He alone ensures
"That you will live in peace and love and never want a thing,
"He only gives He does not take unlike your greedy King.
"And as a sign of His good faith to show His love is deep
"He has performed a miracle and has returned your sheep".
At this the crowd all bowed down low and praised our God on high,
And even I (who knew the truth), a tear came in my eye.

We flew away that afternoon. The sky was blue and clear,
We made good time with chasing wind. Of course we had no fear
Volcano dust would bring us down or interrupt our flight.
We just flew back and soared away at dragon cruising height.

When Honah-Lee came into view I felt a twinge of joy,
Adventuring is very well if you're a headstrong boy
With confidence and fighting talk and actions of the brave,
But dragons like their comforts too: a warm and cosy cave.

I never went with George again. He still roamed far and wide
Righting wrongs and telling folk to keep God on their side.
I heard he'd died in foreign lands when fighting in some wars
That some smart politician was convinced was in God's cause.

That was many years ago but still I can recall
How one man and a dragon tried their best to fool them all.
It's true that even though the plan was daring and was bold
We didn't come back laden down with rubies and with gold
And nor did George win fair maid's hand (she didn't want to leave)
But I know it was all worthwhile for what we did achieve:
My George was made a saint and came a champion of the poor,
And I have made a fortune from this well-paid lecture tour.

Michael Keeble

Wild Words

Words are not always spoken - they are there to formulate our thoughts and afford them expression. To me, many of the most expressive come from the wild; from the natural; from the unfettered and the uncultivated. They are there, expressing beauty, docility, strength, continuity, freedom and much more.

I look in my little garden patch and see the yellowing leaves of my plum tree. They say to me "We have fulfilled our purpose - we have collected water; we have sheltered fruits from wind; we have added grace to your tree and now our work is nearly done - except that we will fall to earth, decay and feed your tree for next year." Continuity is assured. And then, I look over the wall to a holly tree, growing wild, where nature planted it and is giving so much. He has a message to my young plum tree. "You take a rest now - me? I have my busiest time of year ahead -1 nurture my fruits now and they, in turn, nurture so many bird friends. More, I give a haven to those friends on cold, icy, wind-swept days as they hunch among my closely-packed branches and shelter until better times." The holly can be decorative too and in much demand at Christmas-tide to decorate our homes and churches. In the latter, it surely represents immortality and its evergreen quality makes it invulnerable to the passage of time.

'Anchorage' 'support' 'quiet advancement' are all words which come to me - from the wild - when I think seriously of the ivy and how it symbolises those words. And then I think of the carol of the holly and the ivy, and marvel at how the Christian faith has dwelt upon and used this combination from Pagan times, where the holly and the ivy represented the male and female elements of life. It underlines how intrinsic is nature to our beliefs and customs, and indeed our very needs.

The natural world - the wild - comes up with the sense of freedom and the image of beauty in strength. Again, I look to the trees and think of the oak or the yew. The word 'oak' is synonymous with strength and indestructibility. Reflect upon its uses in today's world as divorced as breakwaters on our beaches and as casks maturing our wines. All this with rich, under-stated beauty in its grain. Nature, in her wildness, has given us much.

In my life I need beauty; beauty of form; beauty of nature and indeed, beauty of expression. I can find these facets in so much of the wild and natural. And I look so often to the plethora of trees to afford me the fulfilment of these needs. The sight of silver birch foliage, caught in the wind is very special - it tells me that nature unfolds beauty in the humblest of habitats and the most normal of circumstances - and my heart gives thanks. Look to the weeping willow for sheer grace and beauty of conformation, with the elegant sweep of its long, flowing branches in a gentle breeze. I see beauty in nature given to us, uncultivated as it is, in the glorious mahogany of the copper beech tree. There is real majesty in its vibrant, arrestingly rich colour. And then, the modest familiar apple tree expresses much; there is promise in the oh-so-delicate, yet strong, blossom. The fulfilment comes, expressed in the rounded bloom of the ripe fruit. In the gift of such a universally popular blossom and fruit, there is care expressed; there is practicality expressed and there is popularity expressed.

We are but one species of God's world - given to learn and be learnt from. If we respect the wild and accord it its place, then we may enjoy it and be helped and favoured by its presence.

Margaret Moreton

Star

Once upon a time there were two, early teenage girls. They lived miles apart and never knew each other, though they had much in common. For them both, there was a stable family and equally they respected their elders. They were at that age which saw their awakening sexuality; involuntary blushes were not uncommon. They both accepted their school days and the lessons they absorbed there, though with varying degrees of interest or success. Naturally they longed for approbation.

For Kathy, this came one glorious summer day. She was called from her class and lauded as a master of her craft - she had written a verse or two about the wonder of the sky at night: the ethereal beauty of a new rising moon; the glorious clarity of a dark, cloudless sky, giving a backdrop to a whole galaxy of stars. Her teacher was impressed. He told her that her work had earned her a star. That star, a gold five pointed beauty, was fixed to her work. Star of wonder! It glistened; it reflected her exhilaration - approbation in deed. That star was the half-open door to a possible literary career. She returned to her seat on cloud nine. Her future suddenly seemed bright.

Her contemporary, Katarina, was awarded a star - a bright gold six-pointed emblem. She too had a star which defined her future. Her star was awarded in the company of her family and friends, not because of any excellence in her work, simply because of who she was. It was emblazoned on the lapel of her coat, for all the world to see. He who demanded that it be there intended just that.

An aching train journey followed this award, which took her far into the country, away from what she knew and loved - all because of her star. Journey over, she stood with her family, and that reassured her somewhat. Soon, though, she had to leave her dad and her brothers and go with her mum for a shower. She was filthy and smelly after her long, long journey, so to her mind, that had to be good.

23

That was the last she knew - the Zyclon B did its work and so did the ovens. Her star had truly defined her future. Her Dad, focussing on the giant belching chimney, saw in fatherhood's mind's eye, her star taking its place among nature's galaxies, that would shine there forever.

Once upon a time, no fairy tale this, all this happened: two stars; two messages; two outcomes.

What means a star?

Margaret Moreton

Surreal

Years ago we lived on a Cornish cliff-top, looking out over the Atlantic. In many ways to a Midlander it was idyllic: bracing and sometimes heaving; sometimes swirling and foaming and sometimes mill-pond calm. It was here though, that I came face to face with another's surrealistic, but so calming experience.

I carried out a couple of cups of coffee, to join my husband as he sat surveying the ocean surging at his feet. Far unto the horizon the inky blackness was there, masking its fathomless depths. He thanked me for his coffee, but one look at his face told me to say nothing. He was in another world; he was asleep to the world around him, though with eyes still wide open and fixed eerily on the ocean. An expression on his face I had never seen before; a face so alive and alert was now focussed in the far distance and was detached. I read the signs - I figured he was back with his years ago wartime experience of Atlantic crossings; the bombs; the gun-fights; the sinkings, the swimmings; the drownings; the pick-ups. At that moment he was with chums. Mentally, he had gone down with his many friends, enveloped by the relentlessness of the seas.

He was seeing George who was a builder's apprentice, building a home from the rocks and stone and shells from the sea-bed. "They are splendid bricks," he said. "My lass will love this place," and he was happy.

He was seeing Sam, a garden lover, creating a garden with such flora as he had never seen. He was ecstatic; he thought it was magical. "These blooms are near perfect," he said to himself, "I'll watch them and when they seed I'll harvest them." The prospect had made him smile - his gardener guru would be proud.

He saw his special friend Lane, who had yearned to be an author. This new environment was something he had never envisaged. He could see a veritable library among the rocks. He looked into the crevices which would tell his so much. He had told himself he had so much to write. "They'll love my thoughts about all the wonder there is here. I cannot believe it - why did I never know of its existence?" He led his forefinger to trace out his many and far-reaching thoughts on the sea-bed. What were those thoughts? He would be wondering how life had led him to this new dwelling place and what would it ask of him hence-forth. He marvelled at once at is beauty; its prettiness and even its grotesqueness. Most of all he wondered why he wasn't hungry or thirsty, but he knew he wanted to write. So back he went to the sea-bed and began to assemble his thoughts in the sand. Magically, they were not washed away.

My man took a deep breath. He shook himself. He had seen and mentally spoken with George his builder friend; with Harry who loved things natural and with Sam who wanted so much to be a writer and to share his thoughts with the world. He was giving them back their lives, surreal though they were. He had needed to do that and had done so as if in a dream. Reality now stunned him; he looked at the rolling waves at his feet and the grassy knoll on which he sat, and he smiled for the remembrances and reflections of the friends he had lost years ago.

He'd hoped, in his mind, that they were at peace and he was glad of his thoughtful time with them. "I'll tell her," he said, "I've been with old true friends and how now at last, I have laid so many ghosts."

Margaret Moreton

Dirty Deeds Done Good

Jack choked on his mead as he heard a commotion in the outer office. He swept the nucklebones off the table and indicated the mead flagon to Harold, and the goblets to Ned. They slipped their playthings out of view as Jack sat back into his ample leather chair.

There was a scream from outside. The door banged open and three roundheads rattled in. The captain stood up to the desk.

The guardsmen blocked a swift exit with stamped feet and crossed lances. Not that anyone had legs to run with.

Jack's nonchalant grin greeted the glare. He sucked his teeth.

'Smells like a whorehouse in here,' snapped the captain.

Jack sniffed. 'I wouldn't know.'

'Sir!'

Jack looked around.

The captain, slapped a handbill on the table. 'Is this your handiwork?' he said.

Jack struggled up from his slouch and peered at the object which appeared to be causing some offence. 'No sir.'

'No sir! No sir?'

'Prin'ers 'andiwork, sir. Nice ain't it?'

The captain narrowed his eyes and took a noisy breath through flared nostrils.

'Ow, I gets ye, sir,' said Jack, 'ye sort a means is the rats my 'andiwork, but er...you gid me that job ... so ye kinda threw me at first.'

'Stand up when I speak to you!'

Jack wriggled in his boots. His voice changed. 'I am sir.'

The Captain looked back at his smirking men. He stroked his chin and said, 'of course, just the man for the job. Ferreting the vermin out.' He turned and jutted his chin into Jack's face. 'But you haven't, have you?'

'Well your boys pretty well cleaned up round 'ere. Not left me a lot to go at.'

'When did you last see your Master?'

'Now, that's another question I knows you knows the answer to, sir,' said Jack drawing his left cheek off his teeth. 'It were you dragged him and the Missis out, what, free month ago?'

The Captain's eyes were now a squinting slit. Through gritted teeth he hissed. His looked to his gloved fists as he clenched them and banged them down on the desk. 'He was sprung, you insolent slob. You know he was sprung!'

Jack stood back a little, almost falling into the chair, then up onto his tiptoes. His face blanched. He cleared his throat. 'Do I?'

'Do I? Do I?'

Jack wasn't trying to be facetious. Try offended, Jack. 'Well *I* don't know sir. Who...?'

The captain looked at Jack's two henchmen one at each side of the 'desk' ... table. They didn't look like they could hench much. 'Stand up!' he bawled, 'both of you. Get over there with your master.' He stood back between his two men and three faced three.

The Captain drew his gauntlet across his mouth looking steadily into each man's eyes in turn, before addressing the sentries. 'Like looking into the eyes of fish in a barrel - long dead. Smell like them too, I'll be bound.'

Nobody laughed.

'Are you trying to tell me that, we let you keep your room in the manor house, and the Squire has not been back to...?'

'Very kind of you, it were. Nice it is too ... having it to ourselves...'

'*Our* selves? Our?'

Jack shuddered. 'Well yeah. Not these two, like. Missis an' me sir. Me and Missis. Dint expect me to live there and her back in the cottage?'

'But I did expect you to do something for the privilege, Horner! This is a damned Royalist hotspot. Veritable nest of Papist vipers.' He stabbed the handbill. 'What's that say?' He said pointing to 'RATS, LICE, VERMIN'.

Jack looked at the captain. 'Dirty deeds done good, sir.'

The Captain double checked and glanced at a sentry, who smirked out of the window.

'It - says - rats, lice and vermin...'

'That too sir, yeah.'

'Dirty deeds, *not* done...!' he growled. 'Not done, are they?

'Run off our feet ain't we boys?' He elbowed Harold to stop scratching his arse. 'Printer done a great job and everyone callin' on us to ... look at that,' he said shoving his rat-bitten hand under the Captain's nose.

The officer slapped it away. 'For us who are paying handsomely.'

'We got some good leads, for you, ain't we boys?'

They were all nodding like donkeys.

'Just need to get a ... well don't want to send you in after any wild gooses. That's our job. But, we will get you some sitting ducks...' He looked to his men '...this time next week. How's that?'

The Captain took off his gauntlets.

Jack wondered if that meant business, but what sort - *him* in the rat trap, or the soldiers were going to get comfy? He glanced hopefully at a full flagon on the shelf behind the door.

'That Manor house you are living in: you do know it could be yours?'

Jack thought it already was. That was the deal. He had given them seven houses - well the deeds he had found in the pie - and Lord Frederick had agreed terms. Keeping one was only fair. Did the Captain know? Did he care? Jack wheedled, 'His Lordship ... enjoyed the pie I took him?' He waggled his head. 'Not got indigestion, now I hope - Lord Frederick, I mean.'

That seemed to hit the spot. The Captain stood back, looked at his gloves and put one back on. He raised an ungloved finger very close to Jack's nose.

Jack looked disdainfully at it, as it slowly retreated.

'A week, Horner! Seven days. Same day next week - that's Thursday, but morning, not late afternoon. You had the wits to look into that pie, *and* to bring it to his Lordship. You might not be able to read the word 'deeds', but you know what a Deed is.' He stopped to ensure a reasonable tone, before continuing. He tapped the lose gauntlet on the table. 'His Lordship *appreciated* you bringing him those other six...' he looked all round and coughed '...but if it had been me, I would have you for spoiling the pie in the first place...'

'What and take the pie where it was sent, eh? To one of his nibs Royalist cronies, eh? Eh? I ask you? That what Lord Fred...'

'Calm down man. Of course not. Let's be reasonable.' He coughed. 'Lord Frederick, is a fair and reasonable man, and, well ... we don't want that good nature being taken advantage of now, do we?'

Jack was beginning to relax.

'You *and* me, Jack?' He let the stress sink in. 'That Manor is yours. Yes. The deeds from the ... pie ... are for keeps. His Lordship did in*deed* ... if you'll excuse the joke ... enjoy the pie. He drew himself up to his full height and raised his voice, just a little, 'but he is busy about the Parliament's business, and you must be also.'

'I realise what you are saying Captain, I need to deliver some of my Master's friends, if I am to ... enjoy my slice of the pie and ... live in peace. Yessir.'

The Captain leaned in. 'You pulled out a real plum, there Jack, and don't we know it? But there is a reason why his Lordship let you keep it. Have some nice juice for me next Thursday, else I'll leave with you just the stone. He indicated the door to the sentries and they turned out.

Jack's mouth hung open.

The captain's round-head helmet flashed sunlight from the street as he turned in the doorway and shouted 'That's a good boy.'

Jack clapped his hands, 'Gives me the pip, that bastard', but he cackled and pointed to the new flagon.

'Yes indeed lads, what a good boy am I.'

Kevin Murphy

For my Father on his Anniversary

He brought his children up in Oxford's clean air, away from the smoke of his
industrial home. His three year old daughter fell in the river and was rescued
by some boys.
He could not swim, so built a small pool and taught himself.

He needed better air.
He found it by the waters, with the love of his life,
But it was smoke that killed him.

Water wanted his children,
So he feared it. He feared it and fought it all his life,
But he didn't see smoke creep.

Thames, Isis and Cherwell,
Ditches, delves, Kidneys and quagmire, keen to take a life,
But it was smoke that choked him.

'I'll dig a friendly pool.
My children will jump, splash, swim, beat the water and laugh.'
But he couldn't laugh and smoke.

'Water fought with fire
For me to see the dive, the stroke, the splash and the laugh!
And I see water not smoke.'

He has found better air,
by the water of life, with the love of his life.
Smoke? Water? Breath easy now.

Kevin Murphy

31

The Big Derby

You'd have liked my Dad, your Grandad. He'd have really liked you. Gentle souls the pair of you. Supported the Blades - that's Sheffield United to you. But Uncle Frank was the one who took me to the matches. I knew why like, Mam told me it was the noise, from the war and that. I knew all about the noise ... and how I couldn't make it.

1919 was the last league derby there had been. I suppose it was because they were in different leagues or something. But when I could stand on my own two feet and see between a few people who were taller, me and Frank would catch a game somewhere most weeks.

I didn't find out he wasn't my real Uncle until the great 26/27 season. I'd turned eleven that June and Uncle Frank gave me the Steel City derby for my birthday. Course it wasn't *on* my birthday - it's two games - they play at each other's grounds. That's not at Derby of course - I don't know why they call it that. It's where the two local teams play each other. For us that means when we play Wednesday - the Owls. But that year, Mam said it was the right sort of fever that gripped the city, not like in 1919.

After the games, Uncle Frank would take me into the house and bring my dad a bottle of brown - just the one that they would have to share. The twenties did not roar for us - times were always hard after the war.

We'd all sit down and Mam would corral me - almost put reins on me to keep control. She'd sit there while I rattled off who scored this, who fouled who and 'bloody ref', when Mam would clip Uncle Frank round the ear.

'Don't be teaching t'lad your ways, Frank,' she'd tell him. But she'd smile.

Her hands would go back over her mouth as I prattled on, her eyes intent on Dad, sometimes bringing me up short. I would be beginning to notice the shakes for myself by then. Well I weren't a kid n'more, our Pina, were I?

And '26 had the General Strike in May, and there wasn't such a thing as strike pay, so for my birthday in June, Uncle Frank was giving a present he didn't have to pay for, yet!

The season opened and it was our long school holidays. Us lads would be out on the street being moved on by one set of neighbours after another: 'Stop banging your ball on our wall,' 'watch out for t'winders, lads, get down t'Rec.' The first derby match was one of the first matches of the season - end of August. We had a bit of a trip out and up to Hillsborough on the tram to play Wednesday away. And we won! We beat them 3 - 2.

My, did us lads have something to talk about when we got back to school. And not a few scraps either. It was big school now - lots of extra lads we didn't know and just as many supporting Owls as Blades.

I got a cut lip I was proud of, but you girls don't understand that sort of thing do you? Mam didn't.

Christmas wasn't so bad for us that year. Mam and I had a heart to heart just before New Year. She was pleased with how I'd settled into the Grammar School, and I think she felt she was at last getting someone in the home she could talk to. I see it as my coming of age, even if most people think eleven is a bit early for that.

She was happy how Dad had held down his work this year 'for the first time since the war, really...' She looked into my eyes and took my hands. 'It weren't good for your Dad, the war, you know.' She paused and looked into my soul. 'Uncle Frank is looking after you, i'n't he? Out there?'

I wanted to tell her how many lads and lasses in my class had dads that had simply disappeared in the war, gone to bits, blasted to pieces, ground into the mud, rotted with rats.... But I think she knew I knew all that. She wanted to tell me something else. Something about Uncle Frank maybe.

'Frank isn't your real Uncle, our Eric.'

Was he my real dad?

She coughed and carried on, 'This footie ... Blades, Eric.'

That's why it's him that takes me to the match. That's what Dads do.

Frank had gone and left Dad a cheery chappy, snoozing off a couple of lunchtime pints by the fire.

Mum was happy. Hands holding mine were soft and dry - not gripping and dripping.

'Do you remember your Daddy taking you when you were about five?'

I didn't. 'Really Mam?'

'Yes love, it was the last time they had a proper Derby match.'

I didn't know that Mam understood football. She was a woman after all.

'It was a stinking, rotten, horrible year. You won't remember that either, will you?'

I thought she was going to let me down gently about the Blades in 1919.

'You know about all the men killed in the Great War and your dad ... you know. Well there was this...' Her voice cracked, but she carried on. 'This great plague they called the...'

'Spanish Flu,' I said. 'We did it at school. Killed more people than the war, didn't it Our Mam?'

She looked up to the heavens. 'Cruel, very cruel. But we sailed through it and your Daddy thought, if he survived all that ... mud, he wasn't going to be beat by a bug you couldn't even see. The trams couldn't run properly; your school sent you home some days because there weren't enough teachers.' She chuckled, 'that was after Miss Pilkington - remember her? After she had tried to look after the whole school all on her own, well her and that daft caretaker? What a pair. Never again. Headmistress made a rule you all had to be sent home if they got down to only two teachers!'

She went on, 'the 1919 derby was a like a beam of light the Lord sent shining down on Sheffield at that time. First season after the war was greatly anticipated by the men - and the boys.

'The derby was at the start of the season - and it was to be two weeks running. The first game was at Hillsborough, Wednesday's home ground and they won. There's an advantage playing at home, you know that our Eric. Your own crowd shouts for you and you get a lift.'

We were both nodding.

'Your Daddy's wheezing was a good deal better - it was much worse back then, after he got back from the war. I think the gas must be clearing out of him slowly. It was summer and his wound hadn't given him much jip so he was winding himself up to give the Blades some home support. It meant a lot to him you see. When he had last been, he said it was the last time he was a whole man.'

She swung her head away and back and I saw one hand sweep away a tear.

'We made you after that match.' She blushed, but I knew she knew I was a man now, and would not be shocked.

I'd worked it out with my pal - if I was born in June 1915, then I was made in September 1914. We still didn't know *how* we were made though.

'And the next week he signed up for the Pals Brigade.' She let go of my hands, stood up, went over to the fireplace and put on a log. She lingered, looking down at Dad for a bit, her hand on her cheek. I couldn't see her face. When she turned back she was radiant - almost. She took my hands again and got back to telling me about Uncle not being my uncle.

'That game. 1919. I didn't want him taking you into that crowd breathing all those flu germs, but he was so positive, so strong.' She looked across at him again and he let out a relaxed sigh in his dream.

'He wasn't the only one who had that idea, and there was a good crowd. Your Daddy got you up on his shoulders and you saw the first goal. Unfortunately, you were in the way of a man behind you who happened to miss it. One nil to the Blades and he had missed it.

'He gave your Dad a prod in the back. "Eyup pal!" he starts. Well that was it.

'"Pal?" he says, "Pal? Call me Pal? My Pals are out there in the mud. In the Somme. I 'a'n't got no Pals here." And then he just says "Pal" over and over and over - and he was wilting.

'The bloke sees your Daddy's grey face ... and clutching at his throat ... and beginning to keel over. The bloke lifts you - more or less catches you, actually - and puts you up on his own shoulders. He sees your Daddy is looking out at the game, the rest of the crowd is roaring the Blades on, but Daddy is crying. The bloke doesn't know what to do. Shall he go or shall he stay? Your Daddy isn't going, so the bloke ... this total stranger, who just two minutes before was having a go at your Dad...' She stopped. She blinked away the tears. 'He put his arm around your Dad for the rest of the game ... like two old pals.'

I looked across at my Daddy and dragged a sleeve across my nose. 'Uncle Frank?'

Kevin Murphy
[An extract from his book,
'Convicted for Courage'
written under the name Kevan Pooler.]

Just Be Careful

Bert and Fred were at their local, the Crown, enjoying a pint or two. It *was* Friday night after all. They met up every Friday at 7.30 come rain or shine. The pub was an old-fashioned sort, all dark wood, horse brasses and real ale. Not a piece of chrome in sight, heaven forbid!

They'd already discussed the weather - how the damp cold was affecting Bert's bones and Fred was sick of all the rain, it was water-logging his beloved allotment.

"Now then lad, have you seen George this week?" Fred was only five years older than Bert but insisted on calling him 'lad.' They had known each other most of their lives, having lived in the same small village and then been down the same pit together for almost 40 years, before the place closed down.

George was the artist who lived next door to Fred; he was still regarded as a newcomer to area even though he'd lived there 10 years. He was a fair bit younger than both of them.

"Aye, I have, he were right down in t' dumps, do you know what's up with him?"

"Oh, of course, you weren't in on Saturday with your Elsie, were you? Is she any better now?"

"She's fine now ta, just a bit of a bug, it's going round you know. Anyway, what's this about George?" asked Bert, always keen for a bit of gossip.

"Oh, you missed a right rare treat. Turns out he's been seeing another lass and Chrissy weren't right happy when she found out.

She brought his stuff in on Saturday, in one big black bag and threw it at him. Even knocked his pint over!"

"Ooh heck, who's he been seeing?"

"I don't rightly know, some lass from the city."

"Ohh, you're no good, with only half a tale."

"No, no, no, that's not the end of it, Chrissy's chucked him out completely, he's living at the B&B for the moment."

"So Chrissy's on her own now? If only I were 20 years younger."

"20 years? And the rest lad. But listen, I'm still not finished. Chrissy said she knew something had been up, he's been acting like a right crafty bleeder lately, and then they really got into it She told him not to come home, he was right surprised and begged her not to be like that. She weren't having it though, you could see. Granted she sat there all quiet like while he was effing and jeffing. He told her he was coming home and that was final."

"Ha, I can imagine she went for that."

"Well, nope, surprisingly not. She said he was worthless and she didn't want anything more to do with him. Then she said he was less than worthless, the way he had been treating her for years and then always expecting her to be there. Her parting shot as she left was hilarious, had the whole place in uproar."

"Go on, what did she say, let's hear it."

Fred thought for a moment "Got it, I can remember now. She told him he's a wank stain on the bedsheets of humanity!"

"Ha-ha ha-ha ha!" Bert nearly fell of his stool laughing so much.

"I've never heard anyone called that before. I think I'll just pop round in the morning to see how she is, see if she needs a shoulder to cry on."

"Just be careful lad, just be careful."

Rachel Hilton

Paris

I visited Paris for a few days, several years ago and completely fell in love with the place. I was impressed by the Musee d'Orsay, which is a beautifully converted old train station, housing pieces by Manet, Whistler, Van Gogh, Cezanne, and more.

After that I went to the Musee de l'Orangerie, this houses Monet's eight water lily canvases. It too was great, as the building also had works by Matisse, Renoir and others.

Feeling so enthused, I went to the Louvre the following day. It is huge! Again housing some of the most fabulous works of art and history. They don't just have pictures; I saw crowns made of gold encrusted in magnificent jewels, owned by French kings. I endeavoured to search out the Mona Lisa. I knew she was housed there.

When I found her, it was all a little disappointing. The picture was behind glass, behind a barrier, and with a burly security guard ensuring no one was taking photographs. The picture was a lot smaller than I had anticipated.

Everyone else was 'oohing' and 'aahing' but I wasn't impressed at all. Does that make me uncultured?

Rachel Hilton

TIME

The old man sits by the window
In his rocking chair.
Slippers on, pipe in hand,
Seemingly without a care.

Children walking by
On their way to school,
Laughing, chanting,
Call him an old fool.

Little do they realise
He once was strong and bold.
Now all they see
Is someone frail and old.

He was shipped overseas,
And fought bravely in the war,
It was totally incomprehensible
Everything he saw.

Now he sits in his chair,
Sits and reminisces,
Thoughts of family and friends
And everyone he misses.

Rachel Hilton

Old Ned and Flo

When thinking back, I often relate,
To an aging old couple, that passed by our gate,
Around Worksop town, they'd both come and go,
And went by the names, of 'Old Ned and Flo'.

Ned, he was born of quite noble birth,
But is there a price on what that is worth?
For as he grew older, he had everything made,
But fell in love, with a pretty young maid.

His ma and pa were both quite aghast,
Hoping and praying their love wouldn't last,
Yet try as they may, he just wouldn't hear,
So when they were wed, he was out on his ear.

A home with refinement meant nothing at all,
To this king and queen, who'd answered the call,
A call from the wild, and the wide open spaces,
To shake off the shackles, and throw off the tracers.

A freedom to wander, a freedom to roam,
No longer in future, would they need a home,
For no one was happier, than Flo with her Ned,
With devotion unmatched, from that day they were wed.

In turn each would push, a run-down old pram,
For the comforts of life, they gave not a damn,

Their worldly possessions, were on those four wheels,
And yet they were happy, though down at the heels.

Flo broke her leg, in a fall or such,
So Ned bless his heart, would push his old dutch,
Mile after mile, around country lanes,
The smile on her face, repaid all his pains.

He noted these things, as he toiled in his labours,
For these little moments, were relished and savoured.
As kids we would taunt, and Ned would give chase,
But always made sure, that we won the race.

No malice or grudge, he ever did bare,
For God knows he took, much more than his share,
Now that I'm older, and know I was cruel,
I'd like to say sorry, for playing the fool.

T'was a sad day for Flo, when Ned passed away,
She had no one close, and nowhere to stay,
After choosing the life, of an outdoor pursuit,
It seemed that she now, had to finally take root.

But where could she go, In clothes ragged that smell?
For this was the problem, they knew only too well,
Kindness prevailed at the King Edward Hotel,
They did her up nicely, and treated her well,
Little pink ribbons tied up her white hair.

And she looked like a lady, whilst in their care,
But she never got over, Ned's passing away,
And thought of him constantly, day after day.

Flo died soon after, they say that she pined,
But left us some wonderful memories behind,

If you're up there Ned, with Flo looking down,
I most deeply regret, my acting the clown,
So when the time comes, and my life's at an end,
I hope you'll both meet me, and say. "Welcome my friend".

Pete Brammer

Elvis in My Life

I was *all shook up* when my wife, a *hard headed woman*, *one night* gave *a big hunk o' love* to my one-time mate, Mick Shepherd, or *Old Shep*, as we called him.

As you can imagine, I felt *I got stung*. Apparently he had boasted that she was indeed, *his latest flame*.

Their love exploits had been quite *wild in the country*.

His explanation was: *you can't help falling in love*, and had just presented her with a *good luck charm*.

I became so angry that I yelled at her; "*You're the devil in disguise*."

It is no secret that it has also upset our son's, *Frankie and Johnny*. The youngest, Johnny looked up at me and said *"don't cry daddy."*

All I could say was, *"there goes my everything."* I don't think there has ever been *a fool such as I*. I always knew she was like her mother, *a hard headed woman* who was always guilty of *too much monkey business*.

So now I have the *moody blues* and realised I had to *surrender*.

In the *love letters* I found from her lover, he said:

"*It's now or never - you don't have to say you love me*. We've *got a lot o' livin' to do - just pretend* you love him *until it's time for you to go*. I know he'll have a *Blue Christmas*, but *loving you* means everything to me. *You are always on my mind - I want you, I need you, I love you.* Your husband will always have his *memories*, while we are enjoying a *wonderful world*. I'll always give you my *burning love* and I left the wife telling her *she's not you.*

She sent me a letter begging me to take her back, so I sent it back, after writing on the envelope, *'Return to sender.'*

I'm so *stuck on you* with such a *fever* that *I need your love tonight*. Looking forward to when you *surrender* yourself again to me.
Lots of love,
Hot Dog."

I just can't help believing she has left me. I keep recalling our honeymoon when we had so much *fun in Acapulco*.

Before little Frankie went to bed with his favourite *Teddy bear*, he asked me, "Daddy, *are you lonesome tonight?"* This really hurt me, feeling I had a *wooden heart* - so hurt and without any feelings.

Girls, girls, girls! I've had my bellyful! All I wanted was for her to *love me tender*.

Even my *hound dog Roustabout* seemed to sense my hurt, and ended up chewing my favourite *blue suede shoes*. The house will never be the same again without her - it will be more like a *Heartbreak Hotel* than a loving home.

Several times I've ended up *crying in the chapel* after praying she'll come back to me. I always thought we'd grow old together. Now I'll never be able to *follow that dream*.

Pete Brammer

47

AN EMPTY STAGE

As I drifted off, into a sleep,
A sleep so full of woe,
There came to me the legends lost,
In one almighty show.

Richie Valens bounced on stage,
With 'La Samba' in our ears,
But then he sang his 'Donna'
That brought us all to tears.

Looking on was Buddy,
With an arm 'round Peggy Sue,
While Big '0' stood quite motionless,
Singing 'Blue Bayou'

A roar went up for Elvis,
A song from GI Blues,
Gyrating hips and hair well greased,
And sporting blue suede shoes.

A youthful Eddie Cochran,
With that cheeky boyish face,
Sang about 'Old Shorty'
And how he won the race.

Alma Cogan swept on stage,
 In a gorgeous flowing gown,
With the glitter of the sequins,
Always the talk of the town.

Before the intermission,
Up stepped Nat King Cole,
His voice so smooth and silky,
Though he suffered bless his soul.

His chest and throat were very sore,
Yet his voice it never faulted,
Though it's been so long ago,
Its quality hasn't altered.

How great it was to meet these stars,
Like Dickie Valentine,
To hear him sing with Matt Munro,
So rich like vintage wine.

The Kiss Curl on his forehead,
Though a little greyer now,
Bill Haley showed us how to rock,
With sweat across his brow.

He rocked and rocked around the clock,
As we rose to fever pitch,
Gentleman Jim was next on stage,
His velvet voice so rich.

For me the biggest treat of all,
Being such an ardent fan,
Was Buddy's 'Raining in my Heart'
And 'Dark Eyed Handsome Man'

Last on stage to end the show,
He'd been waiting in the wings,
Bobby Darrin so very smart,
With 'Mack the Knife' and 'Things'

How could I let this chance go by,
Without a souvenir?
So I took myself a photograph,
In my eye a little tear.

The flash of light it woke me up,
As I lay there on my bed,
The realization hitting me,
For all those friends were dead.

Weeks later came a big surprise,
No bigger one, I'll wage,
For when I picked my photo's up,
On one, 'An Empty Stage!'

Pete Brammer

Cabin Ten

Turning towards the clock, ten pm and still twenty-eight degrees.
A dry encompassing heat. Covering her pulse points were chilled
face cloths. In minutes they would be useless.
The AC split system was working overtime. Every so often it silenced
then restarted with a gasping splutter. No doubt delivering insipid
pathogens into the air. Artificial poison everywhere.

She didn't care. As long as it worked now and then, it provided
some comfort. Like a snake sunning itself she lay exposed.
Her mind ran hot with sacred memories.
At four am she rose, letting the taps run to escape the orange desert silt.
Streams of cooling water traced her back, breasts, thighs and stomach.
Her bent neck hid warm salty tears.

At five in the morning the hired Toyota Land Cruiser navigates
her to the chosen spot. Heat beats down on the metal cocoon.
She waits and waits and waits.
He never came. He never would for he was dust and Isabelle
just another mother in pain.

Angela O'Connor

Piccadilly Abode

Left hand cups sunken cheek, right peels back hues of blue.

Swollen pain huddles in the doorway shelter.

TDK glowers, mocking cardboard home.

Animals race past spangled and hooved, loaded with bags of

human greed.

 Hidden person proffers a meat pie past its due date. Dead

eyes take and eat.

The junction witnesses polluted conversations filled with

untold truths. Neon lies.

 Head underground, leave me alone then the circus sounds

will cease.

Damp comfort and a smell of piss. Frozen hands fumble to

deliver bliss.

Needle drops.

   Frown goes.

     No-one stops.

        Angela O'Connor

The Life Model

Stands motionless on a velvet offcut -navy in colour.
Her unsmiling eyes fixed on some point above my head.

Tendrils of auburn hair frame her weathered
heart shaped face - still beautiful.

Acrid dust burns from the old fan, its false heat renders
her pale pink nipples dormant.

Twelve minutes in a shift of weight from left to right.
Determined she remains anchored to the wall.

Arms flank her milky rounded belly.
Finger tips kiss her sturdy dimpled thighs.

Her topaz earrings catch the light and dance
with her freckled chest.

Suddenly she straightens her back mindful of form
Shoulders heighten and bones crack.

Her full pendulous breasts rise in a deep inhale.
I want to be that breath, her breath.

Angela O'Connor

STERLING STUFF

DI Walsh stood to one side and watched as Richard Sterling stepped from beneath the stone portal of the Old Bailey. Flanked by police officers, the multi-billionaire was immediately mobbed by a frenzied scrum of reports and cameramen. Head and shoulders above the hoard, Sterling had a broad grin on his overfed face.

A reporter shouted. 'How do you feel about the results of your case, Rich?'

Sterling presented his pudgy palms to the babbling hoard, but his eyes were on DI Walsh when he said 'I have always had the utmost admiration, confidence, and respect for the British justice system. Under its auspices, an innocent man can take comfort in the knowledge that he will be assured a fair hearing and a fair trial. My confidence in our system has been vindicated this morning. Having been presented with the Fraud Squad's fabricated evidence; trumped up charges, and shoddy presentation. The jury had no hesitation in returning a not guilty verdict. I am an innocent man. The guilty, were my detractors.'

As tall as Sterling, Walsh was leaner and fitter. He was also seething with anger. His anger was not so much directed at Sterling as that of his own investigation team. Some of whom - without his knowledge - had tried to fabricate evidence against the crooked tycoon. The fact that he had no prior knowledge of the illegal methods his team had employed held no water for Walsh. He was in charge of the investigation.

What are you going to do now, Rich! Are you going to sue!?'

'No. I'm not going to sue! What I am going to do is have my chauffeur drive me to the airport. Then I'm going to get aboard my jet and have my pilot fly me to Naples. Then I'm going to take a boat across the bay to Marina de Capri, go aboard my yacht, put to sea, and have one big, wild, celebratory party. I could be away for at least a week!'

On cue a bottle green Bentley drew to the kerb. A uniformed chauffeur unfolded his tall frame from behind the wheel, moved with catlike assurance round the vehicle, and opened the rear passenger door.

Sterling gave Walsh a cold stare, then cut his way through the throng like an icebreaker and got into the vehicle. His aide, Charlie Haines, got in the other side. 'Were you serious about the party?' he asked when the vehicle had joined the light traffic.

'I was. Organise it.' Sterling said.

'It's done.

Sterling looked at him.

'There were two contingencies, Rich,' Haines responded. 'Prison: or party.'

Sterling looked away. 'And what if it had been prison?' he said.

'You wouldn't have wanted for anything.'

'I would have wanted for one thing,' Sterling said, looking back at him, 'Freedom.'

'You have that now. The yacht is ready and waiting. It's loaded with beautiful food, beautiful wines, beautiful drugs, and beautiful people.'

You can keep the drugs, Sterling said to himself. 'Good.' He said aloud. 'That court made me feel dirty. I need to get out to sea and let the wind blow all that dirt away.'

The yacht in question was an eighty metre, four deck Blohm and Voss Golden Odyssey. Sterling had christened her *Sterling Stuff*. She had cost him two hundred million dollars. He had another one on order for his wife's birthday. She and her idiot friends can stay out of my hair then, he thought as he boarded the white and green liveried vessel.

His arrival was greeted by loud cheering from scores of his acquaintances, friends, business partners, well-wishers, and useful hangers on. His enemies' numbers as many. Sterling didn't care. He liked to be surrounded by the mega rich. As soon as his feet had touched the deck, the crew cast off and the vessel put to sea.

They took with them six explosive charges.

The *Sterling Stuff* boasted two swimming pools: a twelve metre pool on the forward sun deck, and a six metre one on the lower stern deck. There were two charges placed beneath this pool: close to the steel flange that secured the prop shaft housings to the stern bulkhead. Two more charges were concealed beneath the twin engines fuel feeds. The remaining two charges were concealed behind the bridge house navigation and steering controls console. Each charge consisted of a battery powered travel clock circuitry wired to one hundred grams of PETN.

Sixty minutes after the *Sterling Stuff* had motored out to sea; the two charges in the lower deck detonated and blew away the stern. Less than a second later, the remaining four charges blew in sequence; ignited the fuel system, and destroyed the communication and navigation systems.

In accordance with the explosive sequence, the stern of the crippled vessel sank rapidly beneath the waves.

The *Sterling Stuff* should have sunk like a stone. But a freak wave hit the rising hull and caused the vessel to turn turtle. Trapped air belched from the vessel in a series of ever decreasing geysers. Then the *Sterling Stuff* settled upside down on the water.

Those revellers who had been thrown into the sea, tried vainly to scramble onto the upturned hull. Those trapped inside the stricken vessel were doomed.

One of them was Richard Sterling.

Sterling was trapped naked inside a shower cubicle in absolute darkness.

The cubicle was rapidly filling with water.

He could feel the shower head beneath his thighs.

He was upside down.

He cried out in fear.

The water was rising.

The sound of his fear terrified him.

He scrambled to his feet.

The water reached his thighs and kept on rising.

He pushed hard against the cubicle door.

But the rapidly growing water pressure was too great.

The door did not budge.

The water reached his waist.

He pressed his back to the door and his hands on the wall and pushed back with all of his considerable weight.

The door did not budge.

The water level reached his chest.

Terror threatened to overwhelm him.

He stood up straight.

The water reached his chin.

He went up on his toes.

The water reached his mouth.

He whimpered.

He pressed his nose against the granite shower tray. I'm going to drown.

But the water stopped rising.

The upturned vessel had settled on the surface of the water.

Maybe I can hold out.

He was unable to bear his own weight.

He took a deep breath and lowered his heels.

He braced his hands against the cubicle walls, went up on his toes, and exhaled slowly.

Time and again he did the same thing.

Could he hold out, until rescue arrived?

Did anyone know?

He felt dizzy and light headed. His arms and leg shook with the strain of supporting his own weight.

I'm going to die.

He thought of all that he had: all that he was leaving behind. The island, the yacht, the plane, the mansions, the houses, the apartments; the global companies and businesses, the billions of dollars, the cars, the race horses, the fine clothes, the fine food, the fine wines, the fine woman.

In his final moment, Richard Sterling thought of all he had in the world.

And he knew that he would gladly give it all away in exchange for just one more mouthful of air.

David R Graham

The Cold Rain Fell

The cold rain fell

But the boy gave no thought to the falling rain
The house was warm - and all was well
And he was engaged with his pencils and his crayon
His mother plied the smoothing iron
And watched a TV show
With half an eye she watch her boy
And marvelled at how quick the plantyn grow

The cold rain fell

But the boy gave no thought to the falling rain
The school was warm - and all was well
And he was engaged with his pencils and crayon
But his thoughts were already on the end of term bell
'Hush now, plantyn,' the teacher said.
'It will soon be time for our short farewell.'

The cold rain fell

It fell on seven tips of slag
That towered above the school
Tip seven soaked up so much rain
Its mass produced a drag
Then - with frightening speed -
Uncounted tons of rain-soaked slag
Slid down the valley side
It formed a wall of slurry-gruel
That struck eight homes - and the Pantglas School

The cold rain fell

But the boy gave no thought to the falling rain
The school was gone - and there was hell
The boy was entombed with his pencils and crayon
Silence fell upon that place - and there did dwell
One hundred and sixteen children died that morn
None would hear again the term bell's knell
In mere seconds - a generation had been shorn

The cold rain fell

It fell on cries of horror wrought from gaping mouth
It fell on frantic mothers rushing to that scene of hell
It fell on miners who responded to the shout
Like a cold and awful blight
It fell on those who laboured to dig survivors out
It fell on the rescue work that continued beneath flood light
Save for the young, and the very old,
Few in the village sought sleep that night

The cold rain fell

It fell on those who wailed and keened their loss
It fell on those who moved about in their private hell
It fell on those who laid flowers in a giant cross
It fell in a trench - where small bodies were soon to dwell
It fell on the shoulders of the NCB boss
It fell on those miners who had known the tips too well

The cold rain fell

But the mother gave no thought to the falling rain
Her boy was gone - her life was an empty shell
She clutched a drawing to her pain -
Her boy had drawn the village - and he had drawn it well
But across the towering mass of slag - in blackest black -
Two fated words the lad had penned: THE END.

David R Graham

FALSE AWAKENING

In the realm of hypnopompia
In transit between wakefulness and sleep
I am conscious that I tread on endless flights of stair
I have no notion where my pointless tramping it will cease,
Nor can I point to any landing and say, 'I started out from
there.'

I feel the rough stone treads beneath my feet
And press the cold and seamless walls,
That hem me to my left and to my right,
And force me up or down these shadowed wells.

In this borderland of consciousness and sleep
My false awakening is a vivid and convincing dream,
Wherein I know that I am not awake
And that my constant treading on these stairs
Is an ordeal I am powerless to forsake.

And yet, within my powerlessness, I know
That I must find a way to free myself
From this constant going up and going down again
And so I strive to hear the breaking power of ticking time,
That will with shrill alarm these stairwells break.

But what price time, when I am not awake?
Time has no meaning here in this hypnopompic state,
Where every sense is radically enhanced and
Witnessed in the rapid movement of my shuttered eyes.
Yet knowing in my dream, that I am still in slumber,
Avails me no advantage or control
For I have no power to rouse myself

From my pointless tramping role.

Up and down these stairs I go.
Or is it down and up? I do not know.
I perceive no purpose to this constant rise and fall
Nor do I know where my ascending and descending,
Will take me anywhere at all.
How long will I endure this ordeals pointless toil?
I do not know. For I perceive no point in time
Where at my travail will be done.

Though I sleep, I am lucid, conscious, sentient, and aware
I feel the stone and sense I tramp these stairs alone
For I perceive no others come or go,
From whom I might learn the purpose of the stair.

But now I sense that time is pressing in
To separate the walls that guide my course
And time brings with it light,
That fades the steps beneath my feet
And makes me fear a fall.

I lurch and flail for something firm to hold
And bolt awake on tousled bedding sheet
Then fall back grateful with relief,
That I am freed from hypnopompia's captivating sleep.

David R Graham.

Free Verse

They said to me forsake your simple rhymes,
Free verse is what describes a poet best,
Those arbiters of taste, those powerful men
The editors who publish poetry today.
That which reminds them of childhood nursery rhymes
Is no longer a measure of a poets worth.
Look more to the poems of Walt Whitman who,
Using assonance and alliteration,
Ensures his verse flows smoothly from the tongue,
And if prose is good enough for some of Shakespeare's work
Then who would speak against such sage advice?
But we know the poetry remembered best,
By those of us who enjoy rather than judge,
Is that where rhyme implants it in our brain.
We all recall verses by the likes of
Hardy, Shelley, Browning or John Betjeman,
Are they and all their kind damned as mere rhymesters
Because some words tend towards a single sound?
While Wordsworth's Daffodils is oft on someone's tongue
His unrhymed Prelude comes less readily to mind.
Yet I cannot escape the need to understand
The secret of writing in this free verse form.
Maybe I could use some sort of subterfuge
And intertwine a rhyme within each line,
So satisfying my urge to versify,
But this would simply be a fools' deceit
To disguise my inability to use
That hidden art which gives free verse its form.
They say my verse must have no set length of line,
No rhymes and no set rhythm too.
They say beware the iambic pentameter,
Unless your verse is to be blank,

So I ask what can I use to drive my words
To the bottom of my still empty page?
They say follow the rhythm of your normal speech,
And listen to the sounds made by your words,
That is when your free verse poetry will come.
This must be the most difficult of tasks for
Those of us taught to live life within the rules.
Experience tells me no rules lead to chaos
It is anathema to the ordered mind.
That must be the secret of this free verse construction
To bring order out of chaos with no set rules.
If no rules exist then how am I to judge
If any of the lines I have written here
Amount to poetry in free verse form
Or just the scribblings of a bored old hand?
But all the while those damn rhymes form and drip
From the corners of my mouth onto the page
Searching for a line they can complete.
But there is no place for them in my free verse
They drift away homeless outcasts on my breath.
What is this more advice you give me now?
You say it doesn't really matter anyhow.
No please don't tell me after all this time
You liked it better when I made it rhyme!

Barrie Purnell

SCARBOROUGH STEPS

*She lives beneath the crying sky pressed up against the foam
flecked sea.*
*In a clifftop house, hugged close by rhododendrons, her clock
ticks away our time.*
She offers you shelter from the approaching storm
Then, when the sun sneaks through the window,
She will walk you through the stained glass dappled hall
To take you on a scenic cliff top ride,
And watch the evening ocean tide,
As she holds you tightly to her side,
While talking of life and suicide
And other truths of which we rarely speak.

She takes you to a church, set down a rain veiled cobbled road
*In which Rossetti clothed the solemn stones with romantic
artistry,*
Where she tells you of those Pre-Raphaelites
And of their lovers and their brotherhood.
Then leaving with downward steps onto the shore
She serves you cake and cinnamon tea,
While the gulls shriek out their misery,
And a rainbow surrenders to the sea,
While she talks of death and poetry,
And other truths of which we rarely speak.

We drove through wooded hills, clad in their autumn leaves
Painted the colour of molten lava by the late October sun.
The tortuous path of the country road hid its ending
Like a metaphor for the enigma of our own lives.
Cocooned inside the car we become philosophical,
Did big bang or God the universe create?
Have we at any time outwitted fate?
Have we souls death will liberate?
Does love all actions validate?
And other truths of which we rarely speak.

She is asking me the question, "what is life really for?
When we have no god to satisfy is love the only answer?"
But I can find no words. My lips are sealed
By the poverty of my own wisdom.
There is little time left to answer this question.
We are near the edge, we are in the queue,
There is nothing she or I can do,
But hold on tight and see it through,
Until the end comes into view,
When all the truths we spoke of are revealed.

Barrie Purnell

Are you Happy?

*We are driving home through slanting rain, a distant shaft of
wet afternoon sunlight drips into my eyes. The rain has washed
the road clean. In front of us it looks brand new, the occasional
rainbow sheen from oil spills the only reminder of previous
travellers. Raindrops race diagonally across the side window as
if desperate to resume their downward journey. Beyond the
rain-streaked windows, the dark green hills are piled up like
melons behind the freshly laid hawthorn hedge. The young
woman driving is the daughter of a friend. Over the space of one
summer she had metamorphosed from teenager to woman and
now sits behind the wheel, with that relaxed confidence born of
youth, in her almost too tight T-shirt and flesh packed jeans. An
avalanche of light brown hair tumbles across her shoulders. The
smell of her perfume mingles with the odour of her damp dog.*

*She is singing along to a CD of Leonard Cohen. I see her face
reflected in the mirror, her tongue, like a small red bird caged
by ivory is framed by full but pale nude lips. Our familiarity had
allowed her to forgo her normal elaborate make-up ritual.
Listening to the golden tones of Cohen's voice the time, like
smooth satin, slips by until the chatter of wipers on the rapidly
drying windscreen brings me back to reality. The rain has
stopped; I open the window, the wind hits against half of my
face and lifts an empty sweet wrapper from my lap, depositing it
on the back seat where it flaps around like a demented butterfly
in the draught. As the rain clouds drift away behind us, the light
seems blindingly white, I put on dark glasses to soften the day
and concentrate on the relative silence. The wind blows in my
memories. I let them travel through my head but they are of no
use to me and I let them fall at my feet. I leave them there for
someone else to find.*

She looks at me with a look of innocence and slight suffering. Her parents had persuaded her to drive me home when she could have been out shopping with friends. "All the songs you like are sad and you write such sad poems", she says, "but sometimes you're very funny. Are you happy?" A question asked out of innocence but requiring me to reach into the uncomfortable regions of my subconscious.

I close the window to shut out the sound of the wind and of rubber on tarmac. "Writing poetry makes me feel good," I reply, "so that's a sort of happy."

I am as happy as most people, I daresay. Happiness is, at best, a transitory state. I am a bit like a sad clown performing in a circus ring of my own words. Sometimes I think I've had too much education and know too much about too many things. Ignorance may be bliss where happiness is concerned. Love is the nearest thing to happy that I've found. How do I know if I am more or less happy than others are when so many people just pretend to be happy?

She interrupts my contemplation. "You've had a happy marriage, and you always appear happy, where do you find all this sadness?"

"I spend a lot of time looking in books," I reply, "but all I really had to do was to look inside myself and listen to other people. I am a dealer in pre-owned despair; I am a dreamer of second hand dreams; I am a thief of other peoples' thoughts; I am a writer of counterfeit conversations." For a moment I think to myself that, if I could steam open her heart, I would steal her dreams and take them as my own.

A frown drifts across her forehead and then the rasping voice of Bonnie Tyler fills the car as she selects another disc. We drive on, both content inside our own world of dreams, hers no doubt centred round her upcoming date that evening and me trying to think back to when I was her age and my optimism was still alive. Back to my youth, back to nineteen fifty seven when I was seeking to lose my innocence, not like now, to regain it. Sometime between then and now I must have lost it but can't remember when or how.

She had not yet had to make the choice between truth and happiness or realized that our happiness can only be measured against the depth of our sadness.

We drive on, racing our shadow, beneath a grey blue postcard perfect sky streaked with high altitude cirrus. The road curls round a row of black poplar trees that are reaching up into the sky as if in surrender. A large wind turbine poisons the landscape, dwarfing the row of farm buildings that it serves but I care little for this defacement. It is but a fleeting visitor to my vision, soon we are past and it isn't even a memory. I am now getting bored and as we get closer to home the SatNav in my head starts to predict our route.

When we arrive nothing has changed. Everything is still as I had left it. I wave her goodbye, she returns to live her life; me to drink again with others in the cafe of lost youth. Happy or not I can't think of a place I'd rather be. I go inside, pour myself a drink and start to write. I feel happy.

Barrie Purnell

Falling in Love takes more than a Kiss

She halted her musing to pause and reflect
On life and it's changes. On cause and effect.
If only she'd realised long before this
It was not what she wanted. She didn't want this
Self loathing and fear during each waking hour.
His mood swings, anger, silence, his power
 Over her life which made her feel worthless.

Then suddenly all became clear.

She could start life again, but on her own terms
Once he had crawled away, down with the worms.
She'd be flat stony broke for no money had she
But she still had her pride and her dignity.
And maybe one day he'd come along,
A friend who'd be kind, gentle and strong
Who would nurture their love, consider her pain
And straighten her brow from creases of strain.
But until that day life would be hers.
To think as she pleased. As free as a bird.
As long as she'd learnt a lesson from this:
That falling in love takes more than a kiss.

Faymarie Morris

The Picture

The child ran, helter-skelter along the lane, the puppy scampering after. He stumbled, his little legs weren't fast enough to keep up with her as blonde pony-tail and black puppy-tail streamed out behind, like pennants. They galloped through a familiar gateway into an adjoining lane that pointed towards the dark wildwood, up ahead. The child started to slow down, allowing the puppy to race on in front but he kept stopping, just to make sure she was still following and also to sniff out nature.

There was a family of rabbits, happy to be chased, knowing he'd never catch them and an old vixen that snuffled behind his ears until he felt thoroughly clean again and mother-washed. A pair of pheasants were unsure of him until he collected a pile of dead leaves together, with his nose, in a bid to camouflage their nest.

Low afternoon sunbeams streaked between the trees as the child stopped to watch a squirrel, with cheeks bulging and tail fluttering, scurrying up the trunk of a chestnut tree before disappearing. She stood on tiptoe, trying to see where he'd gone.

The puppy doubled back to see what the hold-up could be and found her standing, like a statue, staring upwards...

A strange, insistent noise penetrated her brain and she opened her eyes. Where was she? She could sense the damp forest all around her, smell Patch's wet fur and the unmistakable odour of decay. Leaves breaking down, lichen taking hold on fallen tree trunks, mildew, rust, mould and fungal spores spreading, like unseen tree roots...but, this didn't feel like the forest.

A blinding light flashed in her eyes and she wondered if it was the sun. She blinked twice and could make out another, softer light that was shining on the picture of a bright faced child hugging a black and white puppy tightly to her chest, his pink tongue lolling.

Sitting bolt upright, she clutched at the empty air and cried out. She wanted that joyous, carefree other lifetime which was more real to her than this painful, ugly, stiff one.

The welcome aroma of damp woodland was slowly being pushed away by another, less pleasant smell. Stale, cheap perfume mixed with the warm, acrid stench of fresh urine.

"Well, she's done it again. I said she would..." Faraway hands were peeling back the bedclothes, "and she's staring at that picture again. I wonder who the little girl was?"

Ruth knew. Ruth knew exactly who it was but they didn't need to know, ever. Nobody did.

She could feel Patch nudging her hand with his wet nose so she reached out for him. The smell of damp woodland was coming back and she smiled, welcoming it.

Arms and hands started tugging at her, unsettling her, lifting her, pulling at her clothes and then pushing her back down again but she didn't really care what these unknown hands were doing as she went sprinting away, into the woods, after Patch.

He was running faster than he'd ever run before. Away he streaked, back to where the trees were so thick she couldn't see him.

She shouted his name over and over. Lights flashed in her eyes but she hardly even noticed.

All she wanted was Patch and suddenly, there he was. Up ahead. His bright eyes willing her onwards, towards him.

She shouted his name and beckoned for him to come to her, but instead he just stood there, waiting patiently, under the branches of an oak tree. She wanted to smell his damp fur again and feel his soft warm pink belly so she set off, as fast as her legs would go and this time she knew for certain that she would reach him.

And although the dark tunnel of trees seemed never-ending, the child just kept running, helter-skelter, along...

Faymarie Morris

TO SOMEONE WHO CARES

The negative message religions have taught
Is that all other faiths must be wrong
With beliefs not like theirs.
And fanning that flame was the Church's orthodox throng.

Polytheism came long before Christ
When man worshipped Earth's bountiful grace.
When Goddesses of gentleness, nurture and life
Were opposed to the Gods of war and of strife.
We need to rebalance the scales
And make nature important again.
Only then can we see the truth in the signs.
Our judgement will show us the way.

Everything new has been known before.
The oldest of lessons was Mother Nature's lore.
The power of crystals, the stars, herbs and flowers,
Clairvoyance, divining, touch, sound and colours.
Your Goddess can teach you all that she knows
If you'll pass on her message to like-minded souls.
So, relay your knowledge to someone who cares.
Wisewomen of old knew, magic was shared.

I'm not really sure why I wrote this poem but I'm glad I did as its message has had such a profound effect. I had given a copy of my poetry book to a very dear family friend with just a short while to live. He'd had an aggressive brain tumour and spent most of his time reading. He also wrote a daily blog on which he shared his thoughts and feelings with others. I hoped he'd enjoy my book because he'd known me and my family for such a long time, especially my dad. They'd had a great deal of respect for one another.

I asked which poem he enjoyed and was shocked when he said, 'To Someone Who Cares'. He then asked if I would mind if he read it on his blog. I was humbled and would never have guessed it was this poem as he was quite religious.

I watched him reading it on his blog and was deeply moved. He really struggled with the line 'relay your knowledge to someone who cares' so there must have been something about this phrase that affected him. Then he asked if I would mind if his daughter read it at his funeral. Well, of course I didn't mind. It was an honour.

A few weeks ago I met his wife in the supermarket. She told me that every day since he died, 2 years ago, she has read my poem aloud because she felt closer to him. I would never, in my wildest dreams, have imagined that one of my poems could have meant so much.

Faymarie Morris

THE PAST / PRESENT / FUTURE

The Past is gone but always present
The Present is here but not for long
The Future's close and coming fast
It'll soon be here and long since past

They say we should not dwell in the past, for rose tinted glasses, is all we ask, we seek to see, and recall, the memories of those that have long since past, a mum, a dad, a great grandma, a brother, sister or lost beloved, of places, sights and sounds, and special nostalgic smells. We watch old black and white Top of the Pops and think of our youth, and what we were and what we wore, of clothes so extravagant, which are now such a bore. Of suits and ties, of dresses and skirts, of hats of fur and trilby's worn, all that made us when we were young.

As the world did open up, we looked forward to really waking up, chances came and chances went, we missed our boat, as it floated away, we waved goodbye, thinking 'Oh the hell', another will be back in not too long, but when it came it didn't stay long, and by the time we were packed, it had sailed along, and once again we were left in the swell. We sought out partners to live our lives to the full, but along came children, struggle, and domestic strife, of dirty nappies, school uniforms that cost the earth, of ups and downs and a mundane life.

In our mid life experiences, we struggled and strived to survive, to keep a job, food on the plate, the rent paid up and children clothed. Times were hard, and pay was poor, but still we got through it, trying to reach the shore. We put aside what we could in pension schemes that looked so good, had the odd holiday as and when.

After the children had flown the nest, things quietened down as we tried to rest, but the quiet times were far too droll, and boredom set in, the noises were gone, the cries of pain and joy, the Christmas present frenzy lost, the parent teacher meetings in the past, our children in the thrust of life, had almost left us both behind. Our friends and parents dying away left us fraught and about to sway.

But 'Hey Ho', joy to come a well earned retirement, a new life of joy and no more work, a life of perpetual holidays, hobbies, evenings out, oh such joy to envisage.

But 'Woe' its not to be, for our pension pot melted after the freeze, and icy winters are our painful lot, back to surviving as it was, the Past the Present and Future intertwined to a Catalytic compromise.

Robert Tansey

ODE TO A TOWPATH SPRING

'Twas a slightly windy day, cool of nature, quiet of day, cloudy but sunny too, the day we heard the Cuckoo, coo.

'Twas as we rambled down the path, seeking out a foreign lass, the Willow Warbler but no less, that we heard the Cuckoo call.

'Twas indeed a splendid sound, the first we'd heard for several years, but as we listened quite intent, the sound did dwindle as far away, until 'twas gone for the day.

'Twas early Spring, that quite cool day, little stirred to break the spell of loss, when just above we heard a warbling call, and saw a Swallow flying by, along the elongated canal wall.

'Twas once again a gleeful day, Spring was come, and we were there to witness nature at its best, but more was very much still to come.

'Twas as we watched a second swallow fly by low, that we espied high in the sky a circling bird screaming a shrill encore, a lonely figure but majestic too, the Swift had once again come upon our shores.

'Twas shortly after this encounter, that we discerned the tiny blighter, we had sought to find afore, the Willow Warbler, as it flitted from branch to branch, from tree to tree in its entrée, it called aloud its, 'hoo-eet, ee'.

'Twas clear our day out was not in vain, there was as yet so much to see.

’Twas our want at start of day, to seek out badger setts this way, as we meandered down the path to where we knew they were afore.

’Twas overgrown with nettles galore, the bank where one such sett was before, as I clambered down the bank, my foot gave way and down I went, on my back I laughed aloud, but not for long as the nettles scored.

’Twas not to be our badgers homes no more, they had flitted as oft before, no doubt to quieter places be, away from dogs and men like me.

’Twas our second goal that day to seek out Ratty, who’s now rare, thanks to the dreaded demon mink.

’Twas with glee we came upon, a canal bank full of holes, indeed a water vole menagerie.

’Twas by now the end of day, the willows bending to the wind, the air was cooler now than it had been, no insects for the bats to snare, at home they stayed that night we feared.

’Twas to be that home we went, to fireside, and Emmerdale to be depressed, and thinking back to that good day, we’re glad to put Emmerdale to rest.

Robert Tansey

ONE SUMMER'S EVENING

It was a cold summers evening, the sun had gone down early, the sky becoming overcast and getting dark. Earlier it had been pleasantly warm, but changeable, the sun had fought its way through the clouds enough to encourage the family to sit out in the garden for afternoon tea. The children had played by the little pond at the bottom of the garden, and were fascinated by the activity of pond life, midge larva, pond skaters and the occasional plop of some unseen beastie. But as early evening approached, we were inclined to go indoors, that is we adults were, the children seemed oblivious to the encroaching cold, they were intent on continuing in their production of daisy chains on the lawn by the pond, or chasing down the street to the local woods to play hide and seek, or simply search the overgrown lawn for the rare four leaved clover, that we had told them would bring them a lifetime of good luck thanks to the little people.

We adults were settled in the lounge talking, and looking at old photographs, and having the occasional tipple of sherry or port. After a while the children came in and raided the fridge for pop and ice cream or anything else that took their fancy. In order to have some more adult time we sent the children upstairs to play in Rachel's room, they had very soon emptied her toy cupboard, and spread everything all over the floor as their grandma found when she went up to check on them. 'Come on Rachel get this lot tidied up,' she cried, 'What will your mother say to all this mess.' But Rachel said nothing. 'Just a minute,' said Grandma, 'Where is Rachel?' A little boys voice shouted out from the still emptying cupboard, 'She's not here, she never came in, she said she had to do something important.' Grandma stood tall and put her hands on her hips and shouted, 'She should not be out on her own, and besides she'll catch a death of cold out there tonight.' With that she raced down the stairs to the back door and peered out into the darkness of the garden but could not see anything, she listened intently to the sounds of the night but there was not a sound out of place. She had half expected to hear little Rachel singing to herself on the garden seat as she was want to do occasionally when her boisterous cousins got a bit too much for her.

Grandma was by now more than a little worried, she got all the adults to leave the house and search the street and even look in the woods nearby. After an hour or so they all came back, and an anguished and fraught Grandma stood at the front door in a frantic state. They were all by now extremely worried when Granddad said, 'Wait a minute I've an idea.' A few minutes later he returned from the back garden, 'You can all stop worrying, I've found her, but we must be very quiet, very quiet indeed.' He slowly ushered them all into the back garden and told them all to very quietly sit down on the garden chair

As they all did this they saw that Granddad was peeking over to the pond, and as they followed his gaze with theirs, they were astounded by what they saw.

Robert Tansey

EMERGENCY

Come round, lying on the floor. Head hurts –try to get up - can't move. Pain shooting through my body. No use shouting – I live alone - no-one passes my house.

Calm down! Breathe!

In my mind's eye I see an African woman. I remember she said "If we are in trouble, we send a message with our thoughts. We wait, and they come to help". I send a thought message. I am waiting. A key turns in the door and a voice calls "Hi Mum. Suddenly I thought I couldn't wait until the weekend to see you".

Pat Barnett

Snowdrops

Snowdrops
White specks
And green spikes
Come slowly and wondrously
From the dark winter soil.
One day they are hardly there
Then suddenly there are many of them
Peering up from the nourishing earth
Decorating the cold garden border
Peeping through the lawn
Pushing up quickly
Delicate flowers
Dancing

Pat Barnett

LUMIERE 2015

There were thousands of people in Durham on this night, on a pilgrimage, climbing the steep streets to the cathedral. It was raining softly while we stood watching in wonder as images moved over the stone and glass, the music enhancing the sequences of colour and light transforming the building. Then, somehow, we were moving with the crowd towards the cathedral door. It was slow but continuous – we were part of an organic procession, getting closer little by little, until we reached the wide open door and were welcomed in. The building embraced us – we felt the warmth of its age and purpose. Here there was room to expand a little, physically and mentally. Ribbons of coloured light on the vaulted roof flashed and darted, died away and came back reinvented. People sat for a while and looked up, resting and absorbing the experience.

Some lit candles – to give thanks for their life's blessings, to remember those who have passed away, to hope for help for those who are sick in body or mind, and for those who are lost, without family, or shelter or country.

Did St Cuthbert in his holy vault feel the vibration of the myriad feet, and although many stand by his tomb each day, could he have been aware that his church was full of pilgrims, following the light?

Pat Barnett

The Words That We Use

I was sitting relaxing, at peace in our Lounge,
When in came two happy Grandchildren
One said to the other 'oh yep' and I said,
I think it is 'yes' that you mean.
The answer I got came as quite a surprise
Not that I minded, with those cheeky blue eyes!

'No one speaks like you, Grandpa,
No one uses your words.'
'Do you think that is really so?' (I am surprised),
It does sound somewhat absurd,
But then I know I say 'it is not,' instead of saying 'it ain't',
and 'how do you do' 'and not 'aye up' when I am greeting
my friends again.
Apparently in the Twenty-Teens, English is not used my
way.

When I was your age we were taught elocution,
Which showed us all how to speak.
But I guess what it did to the words we then used
        Was make us all sound the same squeak.

'The real thing,' I tell my Grandchildren,
        'Is to understand what we each mean.'
'Communication is what it's about,'
        'And you do really know what I mean? ...I doubt.

Michael Healy

The Pestilential Little Mouse
A sweet little thing - perhaps not!

How dare you come into my house
You pestilential little mouse
You use our home as though it's yours
Upset us all without good cause
Disturb us as we fall asleep
With sounds of tiny running feet
Gnaw the carpets and the doors
Deposit mess across the floors
Be off with you, you little pest
And take away your rancid nest
Go back into the fields you know
Feast on seeds in furrowed row,
For there the farmer, if he sees
You munching on his fresh green peas
Or hiding in his stooks of corn
Will surely, and here I must warn,
Set his cat to seek you out
And that, I am sure I have no doubt
Will bring about the sorry end
Of you my pestilential friend

Michael Healy

Down in the land of Lingtong Boodle

Down in the land of Lingtong Boodle,

Especially in the forest of Lisbet Doodle,

Lives a prehistoric land,

Where dinosaurs feed hand-in-hand.

Lingtong Boodle is a very dark place,

Just not fit for the human race,

With squeaks and creaks and all strange noises,

There is never the sound of human voices.

Bubbling mud and thick smelly fog.

And creatures the size of a twenty-foot dog!

Overhead flies an Archaeopteryx, looking for some prey,

Whilst a Stegosaurus lumbers along, the same route every

day.

With long sharp teeth which rip its food in slices,

The Triceratops watches, a meat-chewing Ceolophysis.

I really must get away from here,

I can feel my growing, shivering fear.

But then I turn in my comfy bed,

And gradually awake my sleepy head.

My eyes open wide, it's all been a dream

Lingtong Boodle? Just my nightmare's scene.

    BUT!!

I pull back the curtains and the sun shines for us,

What's that on the lawn?

        It's   a   TYRANNOSAURUS!!!!!

Michael Healy

MY SECRET PLACE

I have a secret place, behind the garden wall,
Where fears and cares are erased;
It holds me in its thrall.

I lie and watch the birds, as they try to reach the clouds.
There is no need for words
And no harsh sound is allowed.

Breezes caress, flowers delight.
Hedgehog shuffles past, no cause to take fright.
All is gentle, all is calm;
My secret place brings this healing balm.

Such rare tranquility is quite fragile;
Unwanted intrusion leaves my mind less agile.
Leave me alone, with the drowsy drone of the bees.
My secret place is where I find most ease.

Cynthia Smith

SHOP!

Mr and Mrs Kopinski were an elderly couple who owned a little store on Falmouth and Fifth. It sold just about everything and me and my friends loved going there on a Saturday morning. The shop was a veritable cornucopia; though I didn't know long words like that then.

We would stand in front of the line of big candy jars, half a dozen of us from the same class in school, trying to choose between gummy bears, liquorice laces, sherbet dabs, jaw breaker taffy, and lots more. Mr Kopinski was kind and patient: he seemed to understand our dilemma. He had a round, plump, currant bun face, which would crease into such a big smile that his twinkley eyes almost disappeared. When we finally made our minds up, he placed our purchases into small paper bags and took our nickels and dimes, warm from having been clutched for so long.

This was only the start of our Saturday treat. There were dozens of toys for us to inspect and try out, even though we had no money to buy them. Mr Kopinski surely knew that, but it did not deter him from allowing us to run model planes, cars and other miniature vehicles across the counter and around the floor. We would play marbles and skittles and risk wearing out the mechanism on clockwork clowns and animals. It was said that Mr and Mrs Kopinski had no children of their own, which was maybe why they were happy to see youngsters enjoying themselves in their store.

Being a girl, I was expected to like "girls' toys", but found them boring. The clammy plastic skin on dolls felt horrible, and why should I play with replica household appliances like stoves and wash tubs? My mom hated cooking and housework, so why was it supposed to be fun for little girls to pretend they were doing it? It was obvious that boys had much more fun with their toys, so I preferred playing with them.

We liked trying to jump cars over larger vehicles, leading to numerous collisions and triumphant yells. Sometimes I heard Mrs Kopinski's wooden shoes clacking across the floor as she came to check on the commotion. Seeing how much we were enjoying ourselves, she would smile indulgently and return to her provisions counter.

I remember one day at the store in particular. Tired of trying to wreck things, I wandered over to see if Mrs Kopinski needed any help. Mrs K, wisps of white hair escaping as usual from her little paper cap, was in the middle of getting an order together for delivery. Knowing she did not like being interrupted when she was weighing things out, I sat on a sack of flour to wait until she was free.

I was always interested to look at the things which the shop had for sale, even though some of them lining the walls had a coating of dust and so presumably were not popular items. This applied to a bottle of California Poppy scent, which I hoped would still be there when I had saved enough to buy it for Mom's birthday. But the foodstuffs did not stay around so long. There were always boxes of cookies and Hershey bars, tins of beans, vegetables and pet food. Sometimes, towards Christmas time, there would be big fruit cakes, which Mom said you could put the frosting on yourself, so folk would think the cake was home made. I had never tasted most of the cheeses on the counter and, from the smell of some of them, I doubted I ever would. The same went for the collection of evil-looking, dark-coloured sausage.

On the wall there was a large red lobster. Although I knew it wasn't real, its tiny black eyes and drooping whiskers seemed to give it a sad expression.

I had never tasted lobster. I wondered if I had enough quarters left to take one home for Mom, as a surprise for supper. As soon as Mrs Kopinski had finished the order, I asked her excitedly where she kept the lobsters, presuming there was a tank in the back of the store. To my surprise, Mrs K laughed.

"Bless you child, lobsters is what rich folk eat, or those that live by the ocean." She carried on chuckling, as though I had made a huge joke, but patted me on the head when she saw my red face. I hated it when grown-ups laughed at me for something I couldn't be expected to know. Before I had a chance to offer to help behind the counter, the doorbell dinged.

I recognised the portly gentleman who entered as the local bank manager. I had seen him when I was in the bank once with Mom. Disappointed that we had not left with a big bag of dollar bills I wondered why Mom had not asked the manager for some. She said it didn't work like that, unless you robbed a bank. Now there was a thought. Perhaps when I grew up, instead of being a housewife I would be a bank robber. It had to be more exciting than cleaning and listening to your family complaining about what you had cooked for dinner.

Mrs Kopinski beamed delightedly when I asked if I could help her. I went to fetch the tobacco and boot polish that Mr Levy, the bank manager, wanted, and by the time I returned Mrs K was neatly wrapping his other purchases. As usual, she enquired about her customer's health and about his family. Perhaps it was because Mr Levy went on so long about his bad back that Mrs K. appeared less interested than she usually did. When he had left the store, she gave a big sigh and passed a hand across her eyes.

"Oh Susan, I'm so sorry", she said weakly. "I'm a little bit tired. I think I'll lie down for a few minutes. Would you look after the counter for me, dear?" I could hardly believe that I had been entrusted with this important task on my own and waited eagerly for the next customer to come through the door.

As it turned out, I didn't do any serving because the store had to be closed early. Mr Kopinski had come hurrying out to tell me and the boys that his wife was not at all well and he had telephoned for an ambulance. We children were shocked into silence and began to leave the store.

I was just going to pick up my coat and purse when the door bell jangled and someone called "Shop!" A man and a lady in uniform entered with a stretcher. The boys and I waited outside and watched as Mr Kopinski followed his wife, who was on the stretcher, into the ambulance. When it had driven away the boys walked off, but I stood on the sidewalk and cried. Supposing Mrs K died. She was such a lovely, kind lady. (I had completely forgiven her for laughing at me.) Whatever would Mr Kopinski do without her? After a little snivel I felt a bit better and hurried home to tell Mom. Sometimes I was glad I was a girl and did not have to pretend I didn't have any feelings.

It was such a relief when we heard that Mrs Kopinski was not suffering from anything serious and had returned home that evening. Next morning I picked some flowers from our garden and took them, along with a little pot of honey which Mom had got me from the hive, to cheer up Mrs K. I left them on the step in front of the store, as it was still closed and I did not want to disturb the Kopinskis.

When I had told Mom how worried I was about Mrs K, she said the people in the hospital would look after her very well. That got me thinking how wonderful it must be to help sick people feel better. After all, bank robbers spent a lot of time in prison if they got caught, and nobody liked them, but nurses were "angels in uniform". That's what Uncle Harry had said when we visited him in hospital, and I had seen how many boxes of chocolates the nurses were given. Then I realised that the most important people in the hospital were the doctors. It must be amazing to actually save people's lives.

Suddenly my mind was made up: I would be a doctor. And if Mom said girls couldn't be doctors, I would walk over to Granddaddy's and see what *he* said!

....

Those memories are from nearly thirty years ago. The Kopinskis and their store are long gone but I still have fond memories of my visits there. As I sit at my desk enjoying a much-needed break, my pager goes. Sighing, I leave my coffee and go to see what the next patient needs. Sometimes I think life would have been easier if I had been a stay at home housewife, or a shop assistant; but, on a good day, not nearly so rewarding.

Cynthia Smith

Inspired by music Prelude - L'Apres Midi d'un Faune by Debussy.

Born From Nought?
(Almighty Hand)

Born from nought this world of dreams
When all the heavens heaved a sigh?
No mortal ear beheld the screams
That birthed the earth, the sea, the sky!
How then be it men ponder this
And from their musings understand
The empty womb, that black abyss
Of time and space spewed forth the land?
That from its sulphurous choking bowel
Sprang life in bountiful supply
Each plant and beast, each fish and fowl
Then last not least came man, then I?
Now farther take such wisdom hence
Pray dwell on this; foretell the end of time
What justice shall our world dispense
Befitting of all human crime
What answer holds this universe
That born from nought gives substance still?
Entire existence seems perverse
If back into the void we spill
How then be it men ponder more
And musing fail to understand?
Not born from nought, creations core
Was wrought by an Almighty Hand!

Chris South

93

The Clear Out

Where does it all come from?
Boxes and boxes of stuff,
Old papers and files and schoolbooks
Threadbare clothes all covered in fluff.
Where does it all come from?
How I wished I only knew
Most of it isn't mine anyway
So it must all belong to you!
Where is it all coming from?
When will it ever stop?
We've got so much junk to get rid of
Perhaps we should open a shop.

Where has this lot come from?
No! I wouldn't open that box
Well you can't say I didn't warn you
Yes I know it's full of odd socks
What d'you mean they're a little bit cheesy
I used to play rugby in those
Well I thought that I might find the others some day
Look! Please take that peg off your nose.

Where does it all come from?
Why on earth do you want to keep that?
I know for a fact you wont use it
No don't throw away my old hat!
It's got sentimental value
The scarf and the gloves have too.
You can't possibly be serious
About keeping that old canoe?
What d'you mean it might come in handy
It's got a big hole in the bow
And why are we keeping that hideous painting
Those bags of old shoes and the pantomime cow?

Where does it all come from?
What on earth is that under the bed?
How long d'you think it's been there?
Well I'm almost certain it's dead.
I haven't a clue where it came from
I'm not sure if that's fur or mould
Looks like it was some sort of sandwich
Must be at least 2 or 3 years old.

Where does it all come from?
I really couldn't say
I don't recall seeing those before
Did you used to do ballet?
Now don't look at me in that tone of voice!
That tutu would never fit
What d'you mean pink is my colour?
No you wont let it out a bit.
Where does it all come from?
I haven't got a clue
D'you think that were adhesive
To everything: Like glue?
Where does it all come from?
I hope that that's the lot
We must have gone through it all by now
But then again, maybe not.

Where does it all come from?
I think we deserve a rest
We've cleared out the loft and the spare room
The wardrobes and your antique chest
Where does it all come from?
Let's have a nice cup of tea
Then we can start on the garage
Oh sod it! What's on TV?

Chris South

In Strictest Confidence

Chapter 4 My Cuppa Runneth Over, Part one
of Chris' (as yet unpublished) book **The Annals of Warton Tarse**.

"Shhh!" hissed Friar Tetley. "If word of this gets out the whole monastery will want it; and if that blabbermouth the Abbott gets to know of it the whole of Yorkshire will too after his next mass." His companion Friar Tips put his finger to his lips in acknowledgement before looking over his shoulder surreptitiously to see if they were being observed.

"This is *in strictest confidence*, strictest do you understand?" whispered Tetley

"Only me, thee and the Almighty know of this and I'm not sure that even He knows."

Tetley and Tips slunk out of their dormitory amid the snores and grunts of their brothers and slid round the cloisters towards the kitchen keeping in the shadows. Outside the full moon hung low over the Abbey watching them like a big jaundiced eyeball that blinked every so often as a thick swirl of mist rolled up over the edge of the cliff top from the sea below.

"Quick, put that kettle on those cinders!" Tetley bid his partner in subterfuge as they entered the kitchen, "Make sure there's at least two cupfuls of water in it!"

Tips complied keenly.

Tetley dug deep into the left pocket of his cassock and produced a small cloth pouch. He brought it to his nose and inhaled deeply languishing in some sweet yet earthy aroma as yet alien to his companion.

"Can I have a smell?" asked Tips, his nose twitching like a guinea pig at the prospect.

Tetley broke off in mid sniff and eyed him with reluctance. "Oh go on then" he relented handing over the pouch begrudgingly "you'll be tasting it soon enough I suppose, so what harm can a little whiff do?"

Tips, grasped the pouch eagerly, loosened the drawstring and opened the neck, then stuck his nose deep inside and inhaled as though it were his dying breath. Coughing and spluttering ensued with much poking and prodding of his nasal cavity as he tried to extract numerous small particles of leaf and stick from his pointy conk with his stubby finger.

"For heaven's sake man, be quiet!" said Tetley "you're making enough noise to wake the dead."

"Sorry" said Tips "but I seem to have got the sweepings of last autumn up my nose. What on earth is in that bag?"

"Give it here!" Tetley growled, closing it up again. With no explanation whatsoever he poured the now hot water into a wooden pot on the table in front of him and dunked the little bag of sticks and leaves into it for as long as it took him to recite the whole of Psalm twenty three.

"Take it, drink it!" said Tetley handing him a freshly poured cup. Tips looked at the golden brown liquid and sniffed at it cautiously [1] This time his nostrils were assailed by a piquant mellowness with a warm fruity quality that promised forbidden pleasures, reminding him very much of the days of his misspent youth chasing the love of his life Lillian Layman through the bracken on the moors [2]. Hesitantly he took a sip.

The memories came flooding back to him in a wash of passion and emotion so intense that he momentarily spun around expecting a pitchfork to be pointed at his posterior with a ranting farmer behind it. "Wonderful!" he exclaimed before drinking deeper. He closed his eyes and drained the cup. An expression of sheer ecstasy then swept across his visage like a renaissance, his arms raised heavenwards in angelic rapture.

Tetley drained his cup also and gave an energized little shudder before being able to say, "I told you so! How do you feel, can you explain it?"

"Like a new man," said Tips, "Invigorated, revitalised, rejuvenated, born again! I feel ten, no twenty, no make it thirty years younger, yes thirty definitely thirty maybe even more…"

"Isn't it amazing stuff?" said Tetley. "Can you see now why we have to keep quiet about this?"

Tips winked hard and rubbed at his nose, "What d'you call it?" he asked amidst much facial twitchiness.

"I think it's what all men have been searching for through the ages," Tetley boasted, "the fountain of youth, the water of life, The Elixir of Adolescence!" he boomed proudly before suddenly remembering it was a secret. "I call it **TEA** for short." He whispered.

Tips' facial spasms had reached the point of no return "HWAAAATCHOOOOOOO!" The sneeze bounced from pot to pot out of the kitchen and reverberated down the cloisters like all seven trumpets of the apocalypse.

Tetley wiped a snotty twig from his cheek with the cuff of his cassock and discretely put the wet 'teabag' back into his pocket.

Chris South

Footnotes

(1). **Tips was not about to make the same mistake twice and had become suspicious of the fact that Tetley had recited scripture over the drink whilst making it. Although this was an everyday occurrence in a monastery and so was to be expected, the relevance of this particular passage, which speaks of walking through the valley of the shadow of death, had unnerving connotations at the time. There was however a quite simple and ingenious explanation for this. Having brewed this drink on several occasions now, Tetley had experimented with the length of time it took to make it the perfect strength. The Lord's Prayer had proved to be too short and therefore too weak, The Nicene Creed too long and therefore too strong, hence after trying several other passages of well rehearsed scripture he came to the conclusion that Psalm 23 was the perfect length and therefore strength, well for him at least anyway. I recommend finding a biblical text suited to your own personal preference.**

(2). **It was in fact his misspent youth that had landed him in the monastery in the first place. After one long afternoon of chasing and catching and chasing Lillian again across the moors back to her father's hayloft, Tips found himself being chased by her furious father with a pitchfork (after he had come in to get some feed for his cattle) all the way to the doors of the monastery. His out of breath cries of 'Asylum' were eventually heeded by a passing monk, who opened the door just in time to permit access to a flying pitchfork which almost 'kebabed' the Abbott on his way to vespers. For his own safety and atonement the Abbott insisted that Tips become a monk there and then.**

An extract from Innocence Lost by Sarah Carter-Bowden

Locked away
February 1992

She lay there feeling lost, frightened, anxious and so alone. She wanted to shake off the feeling that everything had just been one big nightmare but how could it have been? The evidence was there as plain as day; the four by four cell, the rails on the door hatch and the cobwebs on the lights, although admittedly these could be confused with her own bedroom in the student house she shared with her five friends. On the floor by her bed lay an untouched tray of slop that had been dished up for tea the night before when she'd insisted how hungry she'd been. It seemed like you couldn't get the staff nowadays. Surely the plate should have been cleared away and clearly the cleaner was on strike if the cobwebbed covered lights were anything to go by. The food might have been eaten had it not looked like something a dog had regurgitated and also the horror of her situation made Claire rapidly lose her appetite. She just couldn't face food, certainly not at this time when her life lay in tatters and she could only see a future locked up behind bars.

Claire had not slept at all. Tiredness would overcome her some time later, she guessed, but during the night was when her mind was at its worst. Images swam round her head, violent images that she wanted to shake off and have no part of but still they kept coming, flooding her mind like a torrent, not lapping waves on a beautiful beach which she'd been told to picture when the images fought her. Well, no, today those beautiful, lapping waves would do nothing to relieve the stress, worry and anxiety she felt. Claire had been battling with her mind for years, since her mid teens. The images, not always the same ones, were often swimming round her consciousness. They were always there, either vivid, if they had taken hold of her, or just as a dull memory hidden at the back of her mind. Her parents and close friends had urged her not to think about them and just try to forget them. "They're not real, Claire. You of all people would never do anything like that." But they must have been wrong, mustn't they? The evidence speaks for itself, as here she was lying in a cell on a thin, waterproof mattress, with nothing but a scratchy blanket to keep her warm. She shivered and rolled over to face the graffitied wall that was no more pleasant than the cobwebs she'd been staring at for hours. Clearly the staff on duty had taken their eye off the ball at some point to lock someone in a cell with a permanent marker.

Dawn had broken some time ago. Claire had watched the stream of light gradually fill the room, lighting up the web along with its spider that had scurried away. Claire's only saving grace was that she wasn't terrified of spiders like most of her friends were. At this moment in time, however, another anxiety to focus on would have been welcomed. Instead reality reared its ugly head. She was in a cell with a very long, uncertain journey ahead of her.

Those images that Claire's mind had locked onto during the night gradually began to subside. But only because her thoughts now turned to what was going to happen to her again soon. The police interview room that she had spent most of her time in yesterday was only slightly better than this dank, cold cell she was now confined to. Instead of a spider for company, Claire was faced with two plain-clothes police officers. Neither of the two was pleasant, in fact one was down right horrid. Arrogance oozed from him and every time he displayed his supercilious grin, Claire wanted to slap it right off his smug, fat face. She wouldn't of course. Claire wasn't like that; she wouldn't harm a fly. Having said that, who knows what someone could be capable of once put under immense pressure and stress like she was under at the moment?

The other officer had been slightly more understanding. However, it was clear to see he was following the others' lead. Soon, he would have the personality of 'bad cop' ingrained into him too, certainly if he was to follow the example set by this one. He'd started off the interview quite pleasantly, introducing himself as DC Freeman. The other, Mr Smug Face, was DS Goon, well that was the name Claire misheard. It was actually Groon, only DC Freeman seemed to have a slight speech impediment, either that or Claire's ears were starting to block following her recent throat infection. Claire had to stifle a laugh hearing the name Goon and Goon would be his name from this point on. It certainly fit this burly man's temperament. She didn't like him at all. When she had opened the door of her student house to them, Goon was standing there, his arrogance dominating his frame, which must have been overwhelming because his frame was anything but small. He looked as though he'd been eating his fair share of doughnuts as his belt was bursting at his none existent waistline. Not only was he extremely over weight, he towered over his partner, DC Freeman.

Freeman, in contrast, was very slight. In fact, so slight that Claire couldn't fathom out how he could have passed the rigorous fitness tests set by the police. She knew all about these tests because one of her best friends, Parker, had failed them when he applied to Nottinghamshire Police Force two years ago. Anyway, Claire couldn't see an ounce of muscle on DC Freeman's scrawny body. Although he didn't have a body to be desired, he had a kind face and his eyes twinkled when he smiled. He couldn't have been much older than Claire herself, who had just turned twenty one.

Sarah Carter-Bowden

/